Desert Life

A Guide to the Southwest's Iconic Animals & Plants and How They Survive

by Karen Krebbs

Adventure Publications
Cambridge, Minnesota

Acknowledgments

My heartfelt thanks to the National Park Service for all of their support over the years with my bird and bat research.

Cover and book design by Lora Westberg

Edited by Brett Ortler

Photo credits:

Rick and Nora Bowers: 58, 60 (Mexican free-tailed bat, Cave myotis), 62, 64 (California leaf-nosed bat, Mexican long-tongued bat), 150 (Bisbee beehive cactus) **Phil Dotson/Photo Researchers:** 46 ©**Gary A. Monroe/ USDA=NRCS:** 150 (Johnson pineapple cactus) **MerlinTuttle.org:** 60 (Yuma myotis) **Stan Tekiela:** 60 (Pallid bat), 64 (Lesser long-nosed bat), 68 (Desert pocket mouse, Merriam's Kangaroo Rat) **John and Gloria Tveten/ KAC Productions:** 68 (Desert Shrew).

All other photos via Shutterstock.

Copyright 2017 by Karen Krebbs
Published by Adventure Publications
An imprint of AdventureKEEN
820 Cleveland Street South
Cambridge, Minnesota 55008
(800) 678-7006
www.adventurepublications.net
All rights reserved
Printed in China
ISBN: 978-1-59193-555-1; eISBN: 978-1-59193-664-0

Desert Life

A Guide to the Southwest's Iconic Animals & Plants and How They Survive

Table of Contents

Desert Life Introduction

If you took a flight over a rainforest, you'd be amazed at the beauty and scenery below you. And why shouldn't you be? The rainforest is alive. If the setting changed to a desert, what would you think as you flew over? Many people would probably think they were flying over a barren wasteland. But deserts aren't dead; far from it, they are teeming with all sorts of specialized plants and animals. The Sonoran Desert alone boasts more than 500 species of birds, 130 species of mammals, more than 100 species of reptiles, and more than 2,500 plant species.

And if you spend any time in the desert, you'll see, hear, or smell evidence of all of this life: Coyotes howl during the evening, owls call out, breezes bring the sweet smell of flowers and plants, and it's impossible to miss the towering saguaros, the flowering ironwood trees, and the vivid displays of wildflowers, or the butterflies and hummingbirds zipping from one bloom to another.

This book will introduce you to the deserts of the Southwest and the animals and plants that live in them. Along the way, you'll learn about the fascinating survival strategies and adaptations that help these amazing organisms thrive.

What Is a Desert?

Deserts are usually warm and dry, and many receive less than 10 inches of rain a year. A lack of rainfall isn't the only thing that keeps deserts dry; many have very high rates of evaporation, which means that much of the precipitation that falls never actually reaches the ground. This keeps deserts dry and makes rainfall a rarity. Desert soils are also fairly inhospitable; they often consist of sand, salts, clays, or a specific variety of a calcium known as caliche, which can prevent plants and animals from taking up residence in an area.

The Deserts of the Southwest

There are four major deserts in North America. The Chihuahuan Desert is the largest and covers about 175,000 square miles in Mexico, with fingertips in southern New Mexico, southwestern Texas, and the far-flung reaches of southeastern Arizona.

The Great Basin Desert is our second-largest desert and occupies more than 158,000 square miles; it stretches from southern Idaho and the southeastern corner of Oregon to western Utah and much of northern Nevada.

With an area of 106,000 square miles, the Sonoran Desert is the third largest, and it is located in southern Arizona, southeastern California, part of Baja California, and northwestern Mexico.

The Mojave Desert is the smallest desert in the Southwest, at 54,000 square miles. It covers southern Nevada, the southwestern corner of Utah, part of southern California, and a small piece of western Arizona. In this book, we will focus on the Great Basin, the Mojave, and the Sonoran deserts, as they are primarily found in the western United States.

The Great Basin Desert

The Great Basin is the northernmost desert, and it is both the coldest and the largest of our Southwestern deserts. It receives most of its precipitation in the form of winter snow, and it also boasts impressive elevations—4,000 feet above sea level on average. On the whole, the Great Basin Desert has fewer plant and animal species than our other deserts; nonetheless, the species found in the Great Basin are often specialized due to the area's unique geology. The Great Basin Desert lies between the Rocky Mountains and the Sierra Nevadas, but this area is not one big basin as its name implies. Instead, it has numerous basins and mountain ranges, as well as a number of isolated—and diverse—habitats. The majority of plants found in the Great Basin Desert are grasses or small- or medium-size shrubs (especially sagebrush and saltbushes). In areas where there is standing water, such as near the Great Salt Lake, Pyramid Lake, or Sevier Lake, birds and mammals can be observed, but in drier areas, most of the animals live underground or are difficult to see.

The Mojave Desert

The Mojave is a hot desert; that's actually something of an under-statement, as it is home to Death Valley, the site of the hottest temperature ever recorded on the Earth's surface, an incredible 136.4 degrees Fahrenheit. It's not always hot in the desert, though; temperatures can occasionally dip into the 30s. Nonetheless, there are normally 200 days or more of frost-free temperatures. The desert receives little precipitation—6 inches or less per year. Las Vegas, Nevada, gets even less than that, at 4 inches per year, and Death Valley receives just 2 inches. Most rainfall occurs in winter.

Plant life is usually found in the form of small to medium shrubs, but cacti can also grow here. The Joshua tree is an iconic symbol of the Mojave, and it is seen primarily within the boundaries of the desert. All in all, the Mojave and Sonoran Deserts are inhabited by many of the same plant and animal species, including such plants as creosote bushes, mesquite and barrel cacti, and animals such as lizards, ants, tortoises, Gila monsters, toads, snakes, and birds.

The Sonoran Desert

The Sonoran Desert is also a hot desert, and rainfall occurs in summer and winter. The summer rains often appear as violent, sudden thunderstorms; winter rains are far gentler. Temperatures are hot in the summer, and winters are fairly mild, though freezing temperatures do sometimes occur. Because of its mix of precipitation, the Sonoran is known as a "dry-tropical" desert, and it is home to more species overall than the other deserts found in the U.S. Many of the plants and animals are similar to those found in the Mojave, but there are some significant differences. Unlike in the Mojave, columnar cacti, including saguaro, organ pipe, cardon, and senita, are common here and produce nectar for pollinators. Reptiles are abundant and easy to spot, and while many of the birds found here can also be observed in other deserts, they can be quite numerous in the Sonoran.

The Indigenous Peoples of the Southwest

Indigenous peoples have lived in the deserts of the Southwest for thousands of years, and they've produced distinct cultures rich in story, architecture, and art. Despite immense challenges, these cultures are still thriving today. They have survived, in part, thanks to their deep understanding of the ecosystem, the flora and fauna, and the environment.

An array of distinct peoples have lived in the Southwest at one point or another, and the numerous ruins, pueblos, and even irrigation canals in the Southwest attest to their adaptability and skill at surviving in a decidedly hostile environment. Early cultures include the Hohokam, the Mogollon, and the Anasazi, but they suffered profoundly because of the introduction of European diseases, and this led other indigenous peoples to populate the area soon thereafter.

Since the fifteenth and sixteenth centuries, the Sonoran Desert has been home to a wide variety of cultures, such as the Apache, Pima, Tohono O'odham, Pascua Yaqui, Gila, and the Seri. As the Southwest was settled, the indigenous peoples of the deserts were forcibly removed to reservations by the U.S. military.

The Mojave Desert was (and is) home to the Mohave tribe (also known as the Mojave), who lived near the Colorado River. Today, the Mojave Indian Reservation includes portions of California, Arizona, and Nevada. Four tribes (Navajo, Hopi, Chemehuevi, and Mohave) share the Colorado River Indian Reservation, but each tribe maintains its unique traditions, religions, and culture.

Indigenous peoples of the Great Basin Desert include the Western Shoshone, the North and South Paiute, the Mono, and the Ute.

An Amazing Adventure

Deserts may seem lifeless at first, but once you take a closer look, it's amazing just what you can find: The deserts of the Southwest are populated by howling rodents, insects that squirt blood to deter predators, cacti that are essentially massive water tanks, singing toads, and venomous and nonvenomous snakes and lizards alike. So start reading, and enjoy the adventure!

Desert Safety

Deserts are fascinating habitats most famous for their prickly plants, intense heat, and venomous animals. With a few safety precautions and a healthy dose of respect for the land, visiting a desert can be an unforgettable experience.

Please consider these recommendations:

- Wear a large-brimmed hat. Hats protect your head and also shade your face.
- Wear comfortable and lightweight clothing. Long shirts and pants are good choices. Carry an extra long-sleeved shirt or light rain jacket in case of a sudden storm.
- Wear sunscreen. It doesn't take very long to get an overdose of sun, especially if you don't normally spend a lot of time outdoors.
- Wear hiking boots or closed-toed shoes; sandals are not recommended footwear in the desert.
- Wear sunglasses. The desert floor and sand can reflect back to your eyes.

- Carry a GPS-enabled device, a map, and a compass, and know how to use them. Don't rely solely on GPS or a cellphone.

- Carry at least 1 gallon of water per person per day, and always stay hydrated.

- You should have a first-aid kit in your backpack; also carry a flashlight, batteries, matches, tweezers, a small knife, a granola bar/snacks, and a pencil and paper.

- Do not hike in washes or slot canyons during the summer monsoon rain season. They can flood quickly and without warning, even when there isn't a storm where you are.

- Don't drive into an unfamiliar area unless you have accurate maps; also make sure your vehicle is in top condition and ready for a trip. Tires should be properly inflated, and you should have a spare. Carry additional water/survival supplies in the vehicle.

- If your vehicle breaks down, stay with it.

- Do not feed, approach, or harass wildlife.

- While hiking, watch where you step and sit. Snakes will seek out the same cool areas that you might frequent. Watch where you place your hands also. Scorpions often hide under rocks and in crevices.

- If you are bitten by a snake or stung by a scorpion, stay calm but seek immediate medical attention.

Have a wonderful and safe visit to the desert!

Mammals come in all shapes and forms and eat everything from plants, seeds, and insects to other mammals. In the Southwest, mammals are not especially abundant, as the heat and arid conditions pose special challenges. Nonetheless, some especially hardy mammals are found in the region, and they survive because of their special adaptations for the desert.

When it comes to observing the Southwest's mammals, the key is knowing the best time to look. With some luck, these animals can be spotted early in the day, at night, or during late afternoon. During the peak of the daytime heat, many of the smaller mammals retreat to underground shelters, and larger mammals rest in the shade of plants and vegetation. Still, even if you don't spot them, you can learn about these fascinating creatures and enter into their unique world!

Mountain lion

Mountain lion

Distinguishing Features: Mountain lions are large cats with yellow-brown fur above and whitish underparts. The tip of the long tail is brown or black. The head is small, and the hind legs are long and powerful (and larger than the front legs). The length of the entire body is elongated and built for quick bursts of speed. The ears are round, short, and small. Kittens are spotted but develop adult coloration within six months of age.

Size and Weight: Males can weigh between 100 and 200 pounds, and females range from 65 to 80 pounds.

Mountain lions average about 90 inches in total length, including the tail, which is about 3 feet long. They stand about 2.5 feet high at the shoulder.

Average Lifespan: In the wild, they live from 8 to 15 years; captive animals live longer.

Diet: Lions primarily eat deer, which make up 60–80 percent of their diet, but they also prey upon elk, bighorn sheep, pronghorn, small mammals, rabbits, beaver, fox, raccoon, skunk, porcupine, coyote, bobcat, rodents, birds, and even domestic animals. They also consume insects, grass, and berries. Once they kill their prey, they drag it to a secluded area to be partially consumed and then cover it with leaves, sticks, and dirt for a later meal.

Reproduction: Lions first breed at 2–3 years of age. The male and female come together for a brief courtship period; this mating ritual can last 1–6 days. Most young (cubs) are born in late winter or early spring. The cubs are born with their eyes closed, but they open within 10 days. Females give birth to 1–6 cubs (usually 3–4) and care for the young without any help from the male. The young cats can stay with the mother for up to 2 years, and she will not have additional young until the older young have moved on. The dispersing young don't breed until they have established a home range or territory.

Predators: Humans are the primary predators of mountain lions, which have been extensively hunted. Some lions attack and kill other lions.

When to Look: Mountain lions are nocturnal, but they may be observed in the early morning or at dusk, often near water sources.

Most Threatening Factor: Loss of habitat due to development is the biggest danger to mountain lions, and as humans move into the mountain lion's range, the likelihood of human–mountain lion encounters increases.

Until recently, lions were looked at as a major threat to the cattle industry, but attitudes have slowly changed and most states legally protect these big cats. When lions occasionally kill livestock, wildlife management practices address these particular animals. Some states also have a hunting season to control the lion population. In the Southwest, lion populations are stable.

Coping with Desert Life: Mountain lions are highly adaptable and live comfortably in a desert habitat. They exert little energy during the hottest part of the day, and they are primarily nocturnal, resting during the day in caves, mines, beneath shrubs, in washes, and in other cool, shady areas.

Notes: Lions are solitary, secretive, and very elusive. They also cover a lot of ground; it can take a lion more than a week to travel its entire hunting territory. When hunting, they may ascend a tree and wait for prey to walk beneath it, but they also stalk prey.

When a mountain lion makes a kill, it usually drags the prey to a hiding place. The lion eats the heart, liver, and lungs first. But the intestines and stomach are usually removed and not eaten unless the lion is starving. Lions can eat up to 10 pounds at one time; however, if there is any prey left over, the lion will hide or cover it with vegetation for another time. The carcass may be fed upon for several days as long as the meat doesn't spoil.

Mountain lion encounters, let alone attacks, are very rare, but when you're in mountain lion territory, it's best to be cautious. Most attacks occur on children, so when camping or hiking, adults should not leave young children unattended. Lions have even come into suburban yards and attacked children playing alone. Caution and common sense should be followed when in a wilderness area.

Because mountain lions are nocturnal, it's not surprising that they have excellent night vision. A number of specific adaptations enable them to see well after dark. Their eyes have a special mirror-like layer of reflecting cells known as the *tapetum lucidum*, which is located behind the retina. The tapetum produces "eye shine," which increases the amount of light available for vision; the eye also has numerous light-sensitive rod photoreceptors but very few cones (color receptors). As color vision is useless for most nocturnal creatures, the mountain lion forgoes it in favor of increased visual sensitivity.

Even though mountain lions primarily eat deer, lions also prey on other animals. Mountain lions even eat porcupines, which they usually flip into the air with a paw, disemboweling the prey in the process. But if a younger cat makes a mistake, it can end up with numerous quills embedded in its skin, and this can prove fatal (as the quills work their way inward over time).

How do you determine if a mountain lion is happy or angry? Agitated lions will draw their ears back against the head (this is known as a threat position), emit growls or hisses, and pull up their hindquarters when readying for a leap. On the other hand, if the ears are straight up or forward, the cat is probably in a good mood!

Bobcat

BELIEVE IT OR NOT

Bobcats often consume small mammals, such as rabbits and hares, but they are sometimes far more opportunistic; a bobcat in northern Mexico is famous for snatching fruit-eating bats from the air!

Bobcat

Distinguishing Features: Bobcats are medium-size cats with a short black-tipped tail and large feet. They are larger than housecats, and the backs of their tufted ears are black with a white spot. The fur color is brown or buff with black streaks or spots. The underparts are white with spots or other darker markings.

Size and Weight: Bobcats are about 37 to 40 inches long; this includes their 5- to 7-inch tail. Bobcats weigh between 15 and 40 pounds. Females weigh less than males. Their ears are about 1 inch long.

Average Lifespan: Bobcats usually live 10–15 years. Bobcats in captivity can live 30 years or longer.

Diet: Bobcats are carnivores and prey primarily upon jackrabbits and cottontails, which make up 45 percent or more of their diet. They also eat rodents, porcupines, birds, snakes, and lizards. Sometimes they consume larger mammals, such as deer and bighorn sheep. Bobcats also prey on domestic animals, and they eat fresh carrion.

Bobcats do most of their hunting on the ground, but they will also wait in trees and leap onto prey at times. They have excellent eyesight and hearing and they depend on these senses when hunting.

Reproduction: Females are capable of breeding at 1 year of age, but males usually do not breed until they are 2. Gestation usually lasts 60–70 days; 1–6 young are born (though 3 is a common litter size). Their eyes open at 9–10 days of age, and the kittens nurse for about 2 months. The young can accompany their mother on hunts by the third or fourth month. The young leave their mother and go out on their own by winter or when she breeds again.

Predators: Mountain lions, bears, coyotes, and humans prey on bobcats. Bobcat pelts are valuable to trappers and hunters.

When to Look: Bobcats are nocturnal and very secretive. They are difficult to observe in the wild. Water sources are perhaps the best places to look for bobcats; look in the early morning or late afternoon. They also like to sit on top of rocks and use them as lookouts.

Most Threatening Factor: Bobcats have been hunted and harvested extensively in the United States. As the value of bobcat fur increased, harvesting, also. The majority of the pelts were exported. In the late 1970s, more than 92,000 bobcats were killed in the U.S. for their pelts. New protection guidelines and restrictions on hunting were incorporated (including the elimination of bounties), and bobcat population numbers have improved. Most states in the U.S. now protect bobcats.

Coping with Desert Life: Bobcats are nocturnal and avoid the extreme heat of the desert by resting during the day. They hunt at night. Like most cats, they pant when hot or overheated.

Notes: In northern Mexico, a female bobcat feeds her growing kittens endangered bats! The nectar bats roost underground in an ancient lava tube and leave the roost during early evening to forage on columnar cactus. As the bats exit the roost, the mother bobcat leaps up to catch them or swats the bats to the ground as they fly by her. Because there are more than 100,000 bats roosting in this cave, it's doubtful that bobcats are making a negative impact on the population, but the bobcats sure love the easy meal!

The term "catamount" applies to both the bobcat and the mountain lion. During the days of the pioneers, early settlers referred to both species of wild cats as "cat of the mountains." The term catamount may have been derived from the Spanish word *gatomonte*, which means "cat of the forest or woods." The bobcat gets its common name today because of its bobbed tail and the particular way a bobcat runs (by bobbing or bounding).

When Europeans arrived in North America, they were already familiar with the lynx, which is found in the New World and the Old World alike. Over time, many folk tales, myths, and superstitions had sprung up about the lynx, and the Europeans applied those to the bobcat after arriving in North America. For example, bobcat paws were alleged to cure abdominal cramps, bobcat fur was proclaimed to heal cuts and wounds, and bobcat testes (yes, testes) were used to address pregnancy woes. Perhaps the weirdest "cure" of all was the notion that bobcat scat somehow helped prevent skin from breaking out.

Bobcats are very territorial. The size of their home range depends on prey availability. Their territory can cover as little as 5 miles or as much as 50 miles.

When marking their territory, bobcats create "scratches," areas where bobcats urinate, defecate, and leave behind claw marks. The scratch area is covered afterwards with debris and vegetation. Bobcats often return to scratches within their territory to see if other cats have passed through the area or added to the scratch.

Bobcats have adapted to live in many different habitats. They prefer areas with cliffs and outcrops but also live in open desert, amid thick vegetation, and in woods and grasslands. They often use the cliffs and outcrops as lookout points or as resting areas.

When hunting, bobcats stalk and ambush prey or chase it, then pounce. Bobcats are also opportunistic predators. If smaller prey is not available, bobcats will stalk larger animals such as deer. They usually pounce on the deer's back and bite the back of the neck or the throat. If any of the carcass remains after feeding, the bobcat will hide it to consume later. But coyotes and mountain lions may find the meal and steal it from the bobcat. Bobcats are also excellent climbers and don't hesitate to scale trees after squirrels, birds, or other prey.

Bobcats are normally solitary, but during courtship, males will join the females and mate for days. The usually quiet bobcat will become very vocal at this time, and its screams and hisses are easy to hear. After breeding, the males depart and the females care for the young without any help from the males.

Coyote

BELIEVE IT OR NOT

Coyotes are one of the fastest mammals in the desert. They can reach speeds of up to 40 miles per hour and maintain 20 miles per hour for long periods.

Coyote

Distinguishing Features: Coyotes resemble German shepherds and are often mistaken for them. The fur is buff-gray, with lighter tones on the underparts; the tip of the tail is black. The muzzle and ears are long. Coyotes are smaller than wolves, and their fur is less dense.

Size and Weight: Coyotes are about 47 inches long overall, including the tail, which is about 12 to 14 inches long. They weigh between 20 and 35 pounds; males are larger than females. (On the whole, desert coyotes are smaller than those found in the north.)

Average Lifespan: Wild coyotes live 3–14 years, but captive animals can live up to 20 years.

Diet: Coyotes are omnivores and eat everything from other mammals (rodents, rabbits) to birds, plants, cactus fruit, and berries. They capture small prey by stalking it, then pouncing. In areas where they form packs, they can kill deer and livestock. They also eat carrion.

Reproduction: Mating occurs from January to March and the mated pair can stay together for years. Gestation takes 60–64 days, after which 2–11 pups are born in a den that is found underground or amid dense vegetation. Young emerge from the den by 2–3 weeks but continue to nurse until they are 5–6 weeks old. At around 3 weeks, the parents regurgitate solid food for the pups to eat. The offspring disperse within 6–9 months and can breed at 2 years of age.

Predators: Wolves will kill coyotes if their habitats overlap, as will mountain lions. But in the desert, wolves aren't present and the coyote is king.

When to Look: Coyotes are active throughout the day and night and are often quite comfortable around humans. As long as you don't approach or crowd a coyote it will most likely hang around. But keep your eye on the coyote because it can disappear as fast as it appears! Of course, if you spot a coyote, always keep your children and pets close, and never attempt to feed a coyote or other wildlife.

Most Threatening Factor: Coyotes have probably been persecuted more than any other mammal in the Southwest. Each year, around 400,000 coyotes are killed by humans; they are shot, trapped, gassed, and poisoned, but the coyote is a survivor. Paradoxically, despite being hunted for a century, coyote numbers are actually increasing, and they are expanding their range (even taking up residence in major metropolitan areas). Coyotes have a unique method of coping with the eradication programs established to eliminate them. When coyote population numbers are down, litter sizes increase and yearlings breed at an earlier age. This trait has helped coyotes thrive despite widespread culling programs.

Coping with Desert Life: Smaller animals cope better with heat than larger ones, so it's not surprising that desert coyotes are smaller than northern coyotes. They also have less fur, and it's lighter in color.

During times of drought, coyotes obtain water by eating cactus fruits, berries, juicy insects, and anything else that might contain fluids or water.

Notes: If any animal represents the American West, it's the coyote! They can survive on almost any type of food and can live almost everywhere, including in urban areas and remote deserts.

Coyotes are also thriving because wolf populations have been decimated in many areas, enabling them to move into former wolf habitat. Humans have also indirectly helped coyotes; clearing land for farming and ranching has created perfect territory for coyotes.

The scientific name of the coyote is *Canis latrans*, which means "barking dog." One of the neatest things about being in a desert is getting to listen to coyotes during their nightly howl sessions. Because coyotes don't form large packs, they howl to communicate with other coyotes in the area. The yaps, barks, and howls resonate throughout the dry desert air at night, and just one or two coyotes can yip and yap enough to make it sound like there's a pack of coyotes present. Coyotes are territorial, and the howl sessions help coyotes convey the boundaries of their territory.

Many southwestern Native American tribes (Pima, Navajo, Hopi, Pueblo, and Zuni) have a special relationship with the coyote, which has alternately been described as a trickster, god, hero, divine figure, or savior, involved in the creation of Earth!

According to folklore, coyotes and badgers are hunting partners: The coyote utilizes its keen senses to locate prey in burrows, and the badger uses its powerful claws to dig out the rodent. The coyote and badger then share the rewards of the hunt!

Coyotes have many colorful names, including God's Dog, Song Dog, Trickster, Doctor Coyote, Señor Coyote, Wile E. Coyote, and Old Man Coyote.

Gray fox

Gray foxes are capable of climbing trees and even saguaros to escape predators, find food, or just get a better view of the landscape! They can even jump from branch to branch. The young can climb trees at one month of age. This behavior is very unusual for a canid!

Foxes

(Kit fox, Gray fox)

Distinguishing Features: Gray foxes (tree foxes) are mostly a salt-and-pepper gray; they have white on their underparts, the insides of the legs, the throat, and part of the face. The lower flanks are brownish-red, along with the sides of the neck, the exterior of the ear, and the bottom of the tail. The long tail has a black stripe on the top and its tip is black. A gray fox's fur is coarse and its legs are short.

Kit foxes (desert foxes) are yellow-gray on the back; the underparts are white. The lower legs and feet are an orange-tan color. The ears are very large, and the tail has a black tip.

Size and Weight: Gray foxes weigh 6–15 pounds, with males weighing more than females. From head to rump, they average 19–26 inches; the tail is 11–17 inches long. Females are slightly smaller than males.

Kit foxes weigh 4–6 pounds. They are 31 inches in total length; the tail is 10 inches (about 30 percent of their body length). Females are smaller than the males. The large ears are 5 inches long.

Average Lifespan: Both types of foxes live 4–10 years in the wild. They can live 13 years or longer in captivity.

Diet: Gray foxes eat a variety of small mammals, as well as berries, fruit, and acorns. They also eat birds, insects, and cactus. Plant material makes up more of the gray fox's diet than in other fox species. They also eat carrion.

Kit foxes eat rodents (especially kangaroo rats), as well as birds, rabbits, lizards, scorpions, and insects.

Reproduction: Gray foxes breed December–March and have a single litter a year. Gestation lasts 51–63 days and 2–6 young are born (with an average of 4 per litter). The young open their eyes at around 10 days and can eat solid food in 6 weeks. Young can hunt independently by late summer or early fall.

Kit foxes breed December–February and also have a single litter. Gestation lasts 60 days, and 4–5 young are born. Young (kits) emerge from the den at a month and disperse by the end of the year (4–5 months). Kit foxes may have several dens, often with multiple entrances; all of these dens are used during the breeding period.

Kit fox

Predators: Coyotes, bobcats, mountain lions, and golden eagles threaten foxes.

When to Look: Both types of foxes are nocturnal and crepuscular. You will rarely see them during the day, but you may observe them occasionally in late afternoon or early morning.

Most Threatening Factors: Both types of these foxes have been killed for their pelts. Some states list foxes as furbearers (and therefore open to hunting) and the animals are harvested yearly. Populations have also been reduced by poisoning, and habitat destruction (often tied to agriculture) has also decreased kit fox numbers. Prolonged drought is also a threat, as it makes the vegetation, insects, rabbits, and rodents that foxes depend on more scarce. In a similar respect, pesticides for insects have negatively impacted both species. Rabies and canine distemper can also reduce populations.

Coping with Desert Life: Gray foxes are nocturnal and crepuscular and well adapted for desert life. They den in cool rock crevices, hollow logs, amid dense vegetation, and under rock piles. They obtain moisture from the food they eat.

Kit foxes have huge ears that help radiate heat away from their body, and the hair on their feet protects them against the hot sand. Their small size enables them to cool off more quickly than larger animals. They also conserve water wherever they can; they obtain water and moisture from their food, and their feces are dry and the urine is concentrated. They can also pant, as this helps reduce water loss. They also spend the day resting in their underground burrows.

Notes: Gray foxes leave scat on trails, rocks, and roads in order to mark their territory.

Kit fox numbers decrease during prolonged droughts (those lasting 6 months or longer). During such periods, fewer females breed, litters are smaller, and mortality for the young is higher. But the adults compensate during these hard times by expanding their territories in order to acquire the prey they need to survive; they'll even forgo breeding if things get bad enough. They defend their territories at all times to ensure their own survival.

Javelina

BELIEVE IT OR NOT

Somewhat incredibly, rattlesnake bites do not seem to have any effect on javelinas!

Javelina

(Collared peccary, Wild hog)

Distinguishing Features: Javelinas are hoofed mammals that are similar in shape and size to a pig. They have 3 toes on the rear feet—pigs have 4—as well as a pig-like nose, a short tail and legs, coarse gray-black hair, and pale hair around the collar, neck, and cheeks. Their short, straight canines are razor-sharp as opposed to the long, curved canines found in pigs. Javelinas also have a scent gland on their rumps.

Size and Weight: They are 34–36 inches in total length; the tail is just 1.5 inches long. Averaging 2 feet in height, javelinas can weigh 40–55 pounds.

Average Lifespan: Javelinas live up to 10 years in the wild and 20 years or more in captivity. One captive javelina lived for 24 years!

Diet: Javelinas eat a variety of plant material, including roots, fruits, cactus, nuts, berries, grain, grasses; they also eat small mammals, birds, lizards, and carrion.

Reproduction: Javelina reproduction is dependent on food availability. Javelinas can breed throughout the year, but most young are born in the summer when more-nutritious food is available. Within a javelina herd, there are no pair bonds, and the dominant male mates with the receptive females. The gestation period lasts 142–148 days; 1–2 young are born. They are known as "reds" because they are born red with a black stripe down the back. Reds nurse for about 6–8 weeks, staying close to their mothers for up to 3 months as they learn how to forage. As the young age, they begin to turn gray; by 1 year of age, they resemble adults. Males can breed at 1 year old and females can at 2 years or older.

Predators: Mountain lions, bobcats, coyotes, and humans prey on javelinas. Mortality is high for reds.

When to Look: During the summer, javelinas are active at night when temperatures are cooler, but they can be observed throughout the day in the winter. Javelinas are usually spotted close to water, so look for them near water sources.

Most Threatening Factors: Javelinas require brushy vegetation to survive, so habitat destruction (agriculture, urban development) is probably the largest threat to them. With that said, javelinas are considered a game animal in the Southwest, and populations are stable. Diseases and respiratory problems can kill javelinas, and so can drought; in a dry year, both the mother and her young can die of starvation or dehydration.

Coping with Desert Life: Javelinas rest in caves, mines, rock crevices, dense vegetation, and washes during the heat of the day. Because their fur is coarse and doesn't provide good insulation, they lie together in a group to stay warm when it is cold. They obtain some of the water they need from the fruits and berries they eat.

Notes: Javelinas are very social animals and form herds of 3–18 animals, with food and water availability usually determining the size of the herd. Herds include both sexes, though males move to other herds quite often. But overall, the herd is a permanent social unit and females usually dominate the males.

The word javelina is derived from the Spanish word *javelin* and was inspired by the javelina's sharp canines.

If javelinas are in the area, you might smell them before you see them. The scent gland just above the tail secretes oil that is very pungent. All animals in the herd regularly rub against other members of the herd; they do this to ensure that all members of the herd smell the same, which prevents neighboring javelinas from joining the group. They also rub the scent on trees, rocks, and other objects to mark their territory.

When alarmed or angry, javelinas can raise the hair (hackles) on their head and back, enabling them to look much larger than normal. They also secrete a musky smell when alarmed and clash their teeth together as a warning.

Javelina are managed as a game species, and there is a hunting season on them in most areas. The meat is palatable but the scent gland on the rump must be removed before the meat can be prepared for human consumption. Many ranchers view javelina as a beneficial species, because javelinas can eat prickly pear cactus, which spreads quickly, and most cattle won't eat it. Javelinas keep prickly pear cactus from spreading.

The scent gland on the javelina's back is complex. Several different glands produce secretions that are stored in sacs right below the skin's surface. The gland has a nipple-like opening. Long, coarse, stiff hairs cover the scent gland, but the hairs can be raised when the javelina is alarmed or when marking territory. The scent gland produces a musky, oily liquid that can be expelled up to a few inches away. Young javelinas (reds) do not develop this gland until they are weaned and lose their red body coloring.

The javelina has a well-developed sense of smell, which it uses to detect bulbs and roots underground. While their sense of smell is excellent, they have poor eyesight, and they have difficulty seeing anything beyond 75 yards. They compensate for this with their excellent hearing, which is much better than a human's. When a javelina in the herd hears or smells something odd, all the herd will stop doing what they are doing and then smell and listen. If any of the animals detects danger, they all flee, sometimes in different directions!

Javelinas have complex vocalizations, which include grunting, woofing, growling, squealing, and barking. Grunts are emitted constantly while feeding and by reds, and they are considered a sign of contentment. Adult javelinas woof when frightened or disturbed; growling is a sign of aggression. Young javelinas squeal to locate their mother, or when hungry or playing. Barking is used by javelinas in distress or when separated from the herd. Different tones for each of the vocalizations can also be emitted.

Jaw popping is a sound emitted when a javelina is aggressive or being defensive. The upper and lower teeth are brought together very quickly, and this makes the popping sound. It can be very intimidating to hear this threat in person!

American badger

American badger

Distinguishing Features: Badgers are heavy-bodied mammals. They have grayish-brown fur mixed with areas of fur that are white, black, rust-colored, and buff. The face is black and brown with a white stripe down the middle, sometimes extending down the back to the tail; the head is broad. The legs, ears, and tail are short, and the feet have very long claws.

Size and Weight: They are 24–31 inches on average, and the tail is 4.5–6 inches. Badgers weigh 14–25 pounds. Males are larger than the females.

BELIEVE IT OR NOT

Badgers are fierce fighters when cornered or attacked but prefer to avoid conflicts. If they do have to fight, they are usually the victor. Their bite is very powerful, and their teeth are sharp; in fact, the teeth self-sharpen when they become dull.

Average Lifespan: In the wild, badgers can live 8–14 years, but many individuals, especially the young, don't live past several years. In captivity, a badger lived to 26 years of age.

Diet: Badgers eat rodents, rabbits, reptiles, birds, eggs, snakes, toads, and insects. Food is sometimes buried and eaten later. If a prey item is large, the badger will take it to its burrow and stay underground until it has eaten the prey entirely.

Reproduction: Badgers are normally solitary except during the breeding season. Breeding occurs in late summer or early fall, but the fertilized eggs don't implant in the uterus until later. Known as "delayed implantation," the young (known as kits) aren't born until February. To give birth, females dig a burrow, line part of it with grasses, and then give birth to 1–4 young. The kits are fully furred but helpless and blind at birth. The eyes open after 4–6 weeks and they can leave the den during that time for play sessions. They are weaned at 6 weeks. The mother cares for the young and is quite fierce if anything threatens them. Once they are weaned, the young usually disperse several months later.

Predators: Coyotes, mountain lions, eagles, and humans are all threats to badgers.

When to Look: Badgers are extremely difficult to spot in the desert because they are so secretive and solitary. But they leave a lot of evidence of their presence behind in the form of holes, burrows, and den entrances. Burrow entrances have mounds of dirt in front of them.

Most Threatening Factor: Humans are the biggest threat to badgers, as we're responsible for habitat destruction, as well as the many badgers killed by trapping, poison, or shooting. On occasion, badgers are also taken for their pelts, even though the fur is not that valuable. Internal and external parasites are also a danger.

Coping with Desert Life: During periods of intense heat, badgers rest in their burrows. Burrows can be up to 33 feet long and 10 feet deep. During the winter, badgers enter torpor in their dens for days, weeks, or months at a time; during torpor, the heartbeat decreases, breathing is shallow, and the body temperature falls. The animal survives by living off its fat. Badgers are mainly nocturnal but can be active in early morning.

Notes: Badgers spend much of their life digging and have numerous temporary burrows in their home range and usually use a different burrow each day. The only time that a burrow is used exclusively is when the female cares for the young.

As you might expect, badgers have specialized adaptations for burrowing and living underground. They have a large nictitating membrane (a third eyelid) that protects the eyes from dirt and rocks when a badger is digging. Badgers also have toes that are laced with nerves, indicating that the feet are extra sensitive to feeling and touch. Their long, curved claws are ideal for digging, and the front legs are thick, powerful, and stout. The hind feet, meanwhile, help the badger hurl dirt behind it. All of this adds up to a powerful and efficient digging machine; in fact, they can dig so fast that few burrowing rodents can escape.

Badgers utilize unique hunting techniques, and they are experts at removing rodents and other animals from underground burrows. Badgers are too slow to capture adult rabbits, but they can locate rabbit nests underground by using their sense of smell and their acute hearing. Once they locate a nest, they dig vertically down to the nest to reach the young rabbits. Badgers have also been known to block the entrances and exits to squirrel nests and then dig down to capture the squirrel. Or the badger will wait in a squirrel burrow for the squirrel to return.

A badger's constant digging benefits the environment in a number of ways. It improves soil development by tilling and turning the dirt. Badgers control populations of squirrels, rodents, and snakes. Badgers also dig temporary dens and then abandon them; these old dens are later utilized by other animals.

Desert bighorn sheep

Bighorn sheep

Distinguishing Features: Bighorn sheep are large sheep with a gray-brown color and a white rump patch on the back of the legs and the muzzle. Both the male (known as a ram) and female (known as a ewe) have curved horns. The ram's can be 30–40 inches (along the outside of the curl) whereas the ewe's horns are 10–13 inches. The male's horns are much heavier as well, up to 40 pounds. The horns themselves are yellow-brown to dark brown. Ewes have slimmer necks than rams.

Size and Weight: Bighorns are 60–70 inches long, with tails around 5 inches long. They are 30–39 inches tall at the shoulder and weigh anywhere from 105–300 pounds. Ewes are about 15 percent smaller than rams.

Average Lifespan: Bighorns can live 10–20 years, but mortality is very high for lambs, ranging from 20–80 percent.

Diet: Bighorns subsist on a wide variety of different foods, including grasses, forbs/herbs (buckwheat, Russian thistle), cactus (prickly pear, cholla, saguaro) and their fruits, and plants such as sagebrush, saltbush, and other browse (woody plants).

Reproduction: The mating season, which is known as the rut, occurs in August and September. Dominant rams mate with the ewes, but other males may mate with the females as well. Young gestate for almost 6 months, and 1 lamb is usually born in February or March. Ewes leave the herd to give birth at a safe location (peak, cliff, etc.) but rejoin the group in several days. The females form nursery herds that are made up of other pregnant ewes, mothers with lambs, and yearlings (both male and female). Lambs nurse for 4–5 months. Young rams (1–4 years) disperse from the nursery group and join bachelor groups. The bachelor groups break up during the rut.

Predators: Mountain lions, bobcats, coyotes, humans, gray foxes, and eagles prey upon lambs.

When to Look: Bighorns are shy and very elusive. If you do observe one, it will be at a distance or as the animal is running away from you. Check out mountains and hills close to desert area and you may see a bighorn watching you. Bighorns prefer these habitats for lookouts!

Most Threatening Factors: In the past, bighorn sheep had a much larger distribution than they do today. Habitat loss from agriculture, development, and ranching led to sharp population declines, and bighorns are also susceptible to livestock diseases, including pneumonia, bacterial infections, tapeworms, and mange. Bighorns are hunted—there are dedicated seasons in many states—and poaching also occurs.

Coping with Desert Life: Desert bighorn sheep are very well adapted for desert life. Bighorns possess sweat glands that help prevent overheating, and they also pant to dissipate body heat. A bighorn's thick fur isn't just useful for the cold; it also helps protect them from some of the effects of the heat.

Bighorns can also go a long time without water, up to a week, and they often obtain much of the moisture they need from their food. What's more, their internal organs (stomach and colon) are adapted to conserve moisture within the body, and they produce dry feces and concentrated urine, further conserving moisture.

Like many other animals, bighorns try to avoid the worst of the desert sun, and they seek cool areas (shade, soil, rocks, caves, mines, canyons, and higher elevations) to rest during the hottest part of the day. They can also withstand an elevated body temperature—more than 5 degrees higher than usual—without harm.

Notes: Water and escape terrain limit the distribution of bighorn sheep. When bighorn sheep detect predators, they run for rocky areas, cliffs, and steep habitat, and they graze in areas that are open and free of thick vegetation that might hide a predator. What's more, if water sources aren't in the open, sheep won't drink there. They travel long distances to drink at a safe water source.

When it comes to mating, dominant males have an advantage, so fighting for dominance is a fact of life for males. Males prove their dominance by chasing competitors through ritual displays, as well as through horn clashes, front-leg kicks, and shoving matches. During the horn clashes, rams run towards each other, lower their heads, and hit each other with their horns; incredibly, they leap into the clashes, and both front legs are off the ground at impact. Encounters last for hours, but rams usually emerge relatively unscathed, as their horns and thick skull protect the head and the brain, but occasionally rams are injured or killed during these fights.

Coati

Coati

Distinguishing Features: Coatis look somewhat like raccoons. They have a long mobile snout, a reddish-brown color and a lightly striped tail that is longer than their head and body combined. The face has white around the nose, eyes, ears, and the underside of the neck. The lower legs are usually black and the long claws are curved. The rear legs are longer than the front ones, and the ears are small.

Size and Weight: Coatis are 40–50 inches long with a 2-foot-long tail. They weigh 15–20 pounds, and females are smaller than males.

Average Lifespan: Coatis can live 7–10 years in the wild; captive coatis can live up to 17 years. In wild populations, mortality is high for the young.

Diet: Coatis are omnivores; they eat small mammals, insects, birds, snakes, lizards, frogs, fruits, nuts, berries, eggs, prickly pear, yucca, and carrion.

Reproduction: Coatis live in a matriarchal "tribe" consisting of females. When females are in estrous, a male is allowed into the matriarchal tribe for breeding purposes for a few weeks; that, or the female will leave the group to join up with a male. Most mating takes place in the spring (April). Gestation takes 10–11 weeks. Pregnant females leave the group to give birth in a protected area, such as a tree or tree cavity, cave, mine, or rock crevice. One to seven young are born naked and helpless, with their eyes closed. The females rejoin the tribe after 4–6 weeks once the young can follow her. The young nurse for up to 4 months, with females staying with the matriarchal group. Young males usually leave and disperse.

Predators: Coyotes, bobcats, and mountain lions endanger coatis. Birds of prey also threaten the young.

When to Look: Even though coatis are not considered desert mammals, they can be observed in desert scrubland in winter as they move through arid regions while moving from one area to another. They prefer canyons, riparian habitat, and low mountainous areas that are not far from water.

Coatis are active during the day (diurnal) and easier to observe than nocturnal mammals. They walk with the tail held up vertically (like a periscope!), and you may observe the top of the tail before you see the rest of the animal.

Most Threatening Factors: Diseases can devastate coati populations, and young coatis suffer from high mortality rates. Humans kill coatis, and most ranchers and farmers look at the coati as a pest. Coati fur is not valuable. Water is also a limiting factor for coati populations.

Coping with Desert Life: Coatis are active in the early morning and late afternoon, resting midday when the heat is the worst. They use mines, caves, washes, and shady areas when resting.

Notes: The word "coati" actually specifically refers to the females; "coatimundi" is the name for males. Coatis are also known as "Chulo bears;" *chulo* is a Spanish word for "cocky," a fitting name given the coati's mask-like face and its lumbering, swagger-like walk.

Coatis are very gregarious and gather in groups of 4–30 animals. Tribe members are social and mutual grooming is common among the members. They usually travel in single file order from one area to another. Coatis communicate via grunts, chirps, whines, snarls, and even alarm calls.

When hunting, coatis use their strong paws and their long, curved claws to move dirt and rocks with ease, and they depend on their keen sense of smell to hone in on underground rodents or insects.

Coatis are also often seen in trees; they can ascend or descend them quickly and can jump from branch to branch. The coati's long tail helps it keep balanced, but the tail can't grasp objects. Each coati group lives in a relatively small range, just 5–10 square miles.

Males are not allowed into this exclusive club unless the dominant female approves it. Young males usually leave the tribe by 2 years of age, but they stay as close to the tribe as allowed, only joining the ladies during breeding. Females viciously defend the young against predators. All of the tribe members participate in raising the young. If they do have to fight against predators, it's not unusual for tribe members to work together to fight off a predator or come to the rescue of a member in trouble. Coatis have large canine teeth that are quite sharp, and coatis can be vicious fighters! Nonetheless, mortality is high for young coatis, especially in the first few weeks after they join the tribe.

Coatis belong to the family Procyonidae, which also includes raccoons and ringtails. But coatis are gregarious, diurnal, and form large groups, whereas raccoons and ringtails are nocturnal and more solitary.

The size of a coati tribe depends on the available food resources, the habitat, and the number of breeding females. A tribe consists of females, juveniles, and the very young. A male or males may stay close to the tribe but are not welcomed to the group unless the dominant female allows it. Even then, females dominate the males, and for good reason, as adult male coatis have been observed killing young coatis. Young coatis are also preyed upon by coyotes, foxes, birds of prey, and bobcats.

Ringtail

BELIEVE IT OR NOT

Even though they aren't cats, ringtails are sometimes called "miner's cats" because they once lived alongside miners, who welcomed them in as predators of mice and other vermin.

Ringtail

Distinguishing Features: Ringtails are long and slender with yellow-reddish fur on the back and pale underparts. The face is gray, and they have whitish circles around their large, dark eyes. The tail is ringed with black and white, and its tip is black. Ringtails have partially retractable claws, and their ears are quite large and can move independently of one another.

Size and Weight: The head and body is 14–16 inches long, and the tail is often about as long, usually around 15 inches. They weigh 2–2.5 pounds, with males larger than females.

Average Lifespan: Ringtails live 5–9 years in the wild but can live up to 14 years in captivity.

Diet: Ringtails eat small mammals, birds, eggs, insects, lizards, snakes, centipedes, fruits, seeds, and carrion.

Reproduction: Both the male and female are sexually mature at 10 months. Breeding takes place in spring (April) and gestation lasts 7 weeks. Ringtails den in a variety of places, including burrows, tree hollows, rock crevices, rock piles, under brush piles, in caves, and even in man-made structures. They line the den with grasses, leaves, and mosses, and 1–4 young (kits) are born. Kits are helpless at birth and their eyes open after about a month, which is around when they begin taking solid food. In 3–4 months the young disperse and are on their own. Ringtails are solitary and mark their territory with urine and fecal deposits. Individuals usually stay in the same area for life.

Predators: Coyotes, bobcats, and great horned owls hunt ringtails.

When to Look: Ringtails are nocturnal and difficult to observe. But you may see them in trees, along rock outcrops, and when they cross the road.

Most Threatening Factors: In the past, humans have killed ringtails for their pelts. Today, ringtail fur is not very valuable, so they aren't hunted often. Ringtails are susceptible to rabies and internal parasites.

Coping with Desert Life: Ringtails are nocturnal and sleep in cool dens during the day.

Notes: Climbing skills are a ringtail's expertise! A ringtail's hind feet can rotate at least 180 degrees; this allows the animal to descend quickly head-first and helps make them very maneuverable; they can even travel upside down on suspended ropes or cords, and they often ricochet off objects as they run. All four feet also have partially retractable claws that help them climb, and the long bushy tail helps with balance and to distract predators. (Ringtails also emit a strong musky odor that repels predators.)

Ringtails vocalize to communicate, and their "vocabulary" includes a wide range of sounds, from screams, barks, and growls to whimpers, mews, chitters, and howls.

Ringtails that are taken at a very young age can make good pets. Miners and early settlers often called them miner's cats because they were excellent "mousers" that kept rodent populations down in mines or cabins. Nonetheless, ringtails can also kill chickens and ducks on farms and ranches.

Ringtails will invade both urban and rural habitations and can quickly become pests; they can contract rabies and also have a variety of fleas, ticks, lice, and mites. Nonetheless, they are also beloved by many people; ringtails became the state mammal in Arizona in August 1986.

Ringtails are solitary and territorial, except during the breeding season. They mark their territories with urine and fecal deposits. Male territories may intersect with the females but usually not with other males. Courtship rituals consist of chases, vocalizations, and play fighting. Individuals usually stay in the same area for life but will move from one den to another. Most ringtails spend 3 days or less in a den unless they are caring for young.

Ringtails are famous for their huge eyes, which have massive corneas and lenses in comparison with diurnal mammals. The retinas are almost totally composed of rods, enabling them to see well at night.

Pronghorn

BELIEVE IT OR NOT

Pronghorn are the fastest animals in the western hemisphere! They escape predators by running 40–45 mph, and some sources claim that they can even reach 70 mph!

Mule deer and Pronghorn

Distinguishing Features: Mule deer can range from pale brown and gray to tan or rust; they have a large white rump patch and a small white tail with a black tip. Males (bucks) have antlers that grow upward and are equally forked; their ears are large and wide. Females (does) don't have antlers. Both sexes have white fur beneath the jaw.

Pronghorn are cinnamon to tan in color but black and white on the head and neck. Two horizontal white bands run along the front of the neck, and there are black cheek patches under the jaw. Their undersides and the flanks are both white. The tail is short, and there is a large white rump patch. They have large eyes. Both sexes have black horns; the male's horns are 12 inches long; the female's are 1–3 inches long. Males have a "prong" (forward-facing tine) on the horn. The pronghorn is also notable for its mane, which consists of hair that it can raise and lower.

Size and Weight: Mule deer are around 63 inches in total length; the tail is 8 inches long, as are the ears. Mule deer can weigh up to 350 pounds. Males are larger than females.

Pronghorn have a body length of 40–60 inches; their tail adds on 3–4 inches; they weigh 70–140 pounds, with males larger than females.

Average Lifespan: Mule deer can live up to 10 years in the wild but longer in captivity. Pronghorn live up to 4–5 years in the wild but can live up to 15 years in captivity.

Diet: Mule deer eat grass, forbs, twigs, shrubs, cactus, sagebrush, mesquite beans, catclaw, and jojoba fruit. Pronghorn eat brush, forbs, grasses, sagebrush, rabbit bush, creosote bush, bursage, saltbush, yucca, and shrubs.

Reproduction: Mule deer bucks enter the "rut" in December and January. During this period, bucks compete for females, and the older, larger and more dominant males usually breed with the does. Gestation lasts about 7 months, and 1–2 fawns are born in the summer. Fawns weigh about 7 pounds, are spotted, and hide in vegetation for the first week after birth. Does are responsible for the care of fawns; bucks play no part in raising young. Fawns have weaned by about 4 months and then lose their spots.

Pronghorn enter the rut during late summer (August–September) and bucks may defend harems during this time. During their first

Mule Deer

year, does usually give birth to 1 young, but they'll give birth to twins after that. The gestation period lasts 230–250 days. Young can walk less than an hour after birth; within days, they can run as fast as the adults. As with mule deer, young pronghorn hide during their first few weeks of life in order to evade predators. By 3 weeks, the young are eating vegetation, and by 3 months they share their fur coloration with adults. Females can breed at 15–16 months old; in contrast, males usually wait until they are 3 years old to breed.

Predators: Humans and mountain lions prey on adults. The young are highly vulnerable to predation by coyotes, bobcats, and eagles.

When to Look: Mule deer are active in the early morning and the late afternoon during the summer. Look near water sources.

Pronghorn are active both day and night and especially during the early morning and evening; they are also very wary and shy, preferring open habitat where they can watch for predators.

Most Threatening Factor: Before Europeans arrived in North America, 10 million mule deer were found here. Uncontrolled hunting, habitat destruction, and livestock grazing all reduced the populations to a fraction of what they once were. While populations rebounded over the past century, they still face many threats, including automobiles.

An estimated 30–40 million pronghorn existed in North America prior to contact with Europeans, but hunting, agriculture, and habitat destruction decimated pronghorn populations. In fact, some pronghorn subspecies, including the Sonoran Pronghorn and the Baja California Pronghorn, have almost been driven to extinction.

Coping with Desert Life: During the day, mule deer rest under bushes and in the shade to stay cool. Mule deer have huge ears that can move independently and help them dissipate heat, and they can regulate their body heat via panting. Mule deer also have specially adapted lips that allow them to strip leaves from spiny desert plants without being subjected to the spines.

Pronghorn are well adapted to desert life. During hot periods, the guard hairs on their back/mane can be raised, helping cool the skin. And when it's cold out, these same hairs (when lowered) help shut out the cold. Because pronghorn derive most of their water needs from food, they can also survive long periods without water. If the vegetation has a moisture content of 75 percent or more, pronghorn don't need to drink water at all.

Notes: During the rut, mule deer bucks undergo many physiological changes. Their antlers become full grown, their necks and shoulders swell, they become hyperactive and aggressive, and the buck's food intake drastically decreases or ceases. Bucks then fight for the privilege to breed with does. Once the mating period is over, bucks drop their antlers and begin growing new ones for the next rut.

Pronghorn are famous for their blazing speed; they can sometimes reach 55 miles per hour, and, incredibly, they can maintain high speeds for long distances.

Black-tailed jackrabbit

Rabbits and Hares

(Audubon's cottontail, California jackrabbit)

Distinguishing Features: Desert cottontails are small- or medium-size rabbits with large eyes and buff-gray coloration on the back, sides, and face. The shoulders and legs are darker; the rear legs are larger and longer than the front legs. The tail is gray-black above and white below. The whiskers are black and the hind legs are longer than the front legs.

Black-tailed jackrabbits are large rabbits with big eyes; they are light gray along the back and face and have lighter underparts. The ears are tipped with black; the top of the tail is black, and the bottom of it is white. As with the desert cottontail, the black-tailed jackrabbit's rear legs are longer than the front legs.

Size and Weight: The desert cottontail is 15–16 inches long, including its tail, which is 1–2 inches long. The ears are 2–3 inches long. Desert cottontails weigh about 1.5–3 pounds; females are larger than males.

Black-tailed jackrabbits are 24 inches long in total; the ears are 6 inches long, and the tail is 2–3.5 inches long. They weigh 3–7 pounds.

Average Lifespan: Most rabbits and hares live just a few years, but they can live longer in captivity, up to 6–7 years.

Diet: Rabbits and hares eat grass, leaves, forbs, shrubs, roots, green vegetation, mesquite, palo verde, yucca, acacias, catclaw, and prickly pear.

Reproduction: Desert cottontails can breed as early as 3 months of age, and it is not uncommon for cottontails to breed several times a year. Gestation lasts 28–30 days, and litters consist of 2–4 young. The young are born in a nest of grass and fur that is located in a depression on the ground. The young are weaned in 2–3 weeks. Sexual maturity is reached as early as 80 days.

Black-tailed jackrabbits can also breed 3–4 times a year and before they are a year old, but some wait until they are a year old to breed. Gestation lasts 41–47 days and 1–6 leverets (young hares) are born. The leverets are born in a nest that may consist of fur and vegetation; it is usually located in a slight depression on the ground.

Predators: Coyotes, bobcat, foxes, badgers, birds of prey, and snakes are a threat.

When to Look: Look for rabbits and hares early in the morning, late afternoon, and during the evening. Both of these animals are fairly easy to spot.

Most Threatening Factor: Humans kill rabbits and hares for food, for pelts, and amid recreational hunting.

Coping with Desert Life: Both the desert cottontail and the black-tailed jackrabbit are well adapted for desert life. Both avoid the daytime heat and obtain most of the water they require from their food, so they aren't dependent on sources of open water. Their waste products are also concentrated and contain little water.

Both species also have light-colored fur that reflects light, and their ears act as heat dispersers; incredibly, the veins inside the ears can dilate, allowing them to disperse up to one-third of their body heat. (For this reason, they will often sit with the ears up and face the oncoming wind or breeze to cool off.) Jackrabbits can even store heat during the day via a temporarily raised body temperature and then release it at night.

Notes: Young jackrabbits are called hares. The young are born with thick fur and with their eyes open; they can follow their mother almost immediately. Cottontails, on the other hand, give birth to naked, helpless young that can't open their eyes at birth.

If natural predators of rabbits and hares are reduced or eliminated, rabbit and hare populations can increase dramatically, leading to serious damage to agriculture and orchards.

Jackrabbits have powerful eyes and ears, and they are constantly aware of potential predators. If they detect a threat, they stand on their hind legs to get a better view, and if they spot a threat, they can run incredibly quickly, up to 40 miles per hour. When a rabbit takes off, many predators give up before the race is run.

Jackrabbits prefer deserts and grasslands with little cover or a habitat with shrubs, which they use during the day for shade, cover, and to hide from predators. They also rest in shallow dirt depressions during the day. Jackrabbits survive despite subsisting on plants that most other animals avoid. Creosote bush is an example; most herbivores avoid it, but jackrabbits eat it often. Overgrazed land enhances habitat for jackrabbits, because shrubs are the dominant plant species in such areas.

Jackrabbits usually outrun predators with ease, but coyotes can run down jackrabbits by taking multiple turns, which tires the jackrabbit out. They also ambush rabbits. Jackrabbits are eaten by humans, but rabbits can carry bubonic plague and other diseases that can be transmitted to humans, so eat at your own risk!

Cottontails escape predators by running and then hiding in their burrows. Cottontails use burrows that have been abandoned by skunks, badgers, foxes, and others. They also hide under rocks and beneath thick vegetation.

Cottontails have excellent hearing, thanks to the large bones in their middle ear and the dry air of the desert. Cottontails don't favor wind or rain, as it interferes with their hearing and sense of smell. They prefer to travel and feed on still days when their senses are most acute.

Western pipistrelle

Widespread Bats

(Mexican free-tailed bat, Pallid bat, Western pipistrelles, Yuma myotis, Cave myotis)

Distinguishing Features: Mexican free-tailed bats have brown-gray hair and wrinkled lips. The ears do not join in the middle; the tail is long and free of a tail membrane.

Pallid bats are light-colored with yellow or tan fur and huge pink ears. The glands on the face produce a unique odor.

Western pipistrelles have light brown–tan fur and a black mask. The small ears have a blunt curved prominence in front of the opening of the ear (this is called a tragus).

Yuma myotis have light brown fur and are a similar color on the face and muzzle. They have small ears and a long prominence at the opening of the ear.

Cave myotis have light brown or gray fur and small ears with a long prominence at the ear opening. They have a bald spot between the shoulders.

Size and Weight:

Bat Species and Measurements	Total Length (Inches)	Tail (Inches)	Ear (Inches)	Forearm (Inches)	Weight (Ounces)
Mexican free-tailed bat	4	1.3	0.7	1.26–1.79	0.4
Pallid bat	2.7	1.8	1.2	1.95–2.14	0.7
Western pipistrelle	2.8	1.3	0.5	1.0–1.29	0.1
Yuma myotis	3.1	1.3	0.5	1.17–1.40	0.3
Cave myotis	4.5	1.6	0.6	1.56–1.75	0.5

Average Lifespan: Many bats die during their first year of life, but if they survive, they can live 10–30 years.

Diet: All of these species are insectivores and eat a variety of insects (mosquitoes, flying ants, moths, termites, katydids, etc.). Pallid bats also eat scorpions, beetles, grasshoppers, and crickets.

Reproduction: Because many bats hibernate to avoid winter temperatures, reproduction has to coincide with their hibernation schedule. Female pallid bats, Western pipistrelles, cave myotis, and Yuma myotis

Mexican free-tailed bat

Pallid bat

Yuma myotis

Cave myotis

store sperm for fertilization later and have delayed ovulation. For these bats, mating occurs in late summer or early fall and prior to hibernation. When the females emerge from hibernation in the spring, their eggs are released and the stored sperm fertilizes them. This way the female can sleep during the winter and not utilize the precious energy it takes to produce unborn young! Male Mexican free-tailed bats even store sperm themselves so they are ready to breed in the spring with females that did not store sperm! Breeding in late summer also ensures that the bats are at their physical best before hibernating.

Predators: Owls, snakes, raptors, raccoons, bobcats, and coyotes prey on bats.

When to Look: All insectivorous bats are nocturnal and can be observed around lights as they capture insects. If flying insects are out and about, you will see bats chasing them!

Most Threatening Factor: Humans are the greatest threat to bats. Bats are killed in their roosts, poisoned by pesticides, and their habitat is often destroyed. Pallid bats spend a lot of time on the ground and can be accidentally caught in rodent traps.

Coping with Desert Life: Even though insect prey provides a lot of moisture, most bats require additional water to survive in the desert. But because bats can fly, finding water is fairly easy. Better yet, because they are nocturnal, they avoid the heat of the day, instead resting in their cool roosts.

Notes: Bats that feed on insects can "see" via sound. Known as echo-location, this adaptation enables them to safely navigate and capture prey in the dark. Bats emit a sound orally or nasally and the brain processes the echo, allowing the bat to detect the size, shape, speed, direction, and even the texture of the insect being pursued.

When bats echolocate, it's usually beyond the range of human hearing, but some species—known as whispering bats—echolocate at frequencies humans can hear. These bats produce five pulses per second to begin with, but they rev up to 200 pulses per second when they detect an insect and go in for the kill. (This is known as a feeding buzz.) In the end, not many insects survive this efficient predator!

Pallid bats have large eyes and have excellent vision in low light; they can also see ultraviolet light, a handy trait given that one of their major prey items (scorpions) glows under UV light. Insectivorous (insect-eating) bats have small eyes but probably see as well as humans. Nectar and fruit bats have large eyes and excellent vision.

Big free-tailed bat

Rarer Bats

(Big free-tailed bat, California leaf-nosed bat, Townsend's big-eared bat, Lesser long-nosed bat, Mexican long-tongued bat)

Distinguishing Features: Big free-tailed bats have large, broad ears that are joined at the midline of the head, and they also have vertical wrinkles on the lips. The tail extends beyond the tail membrane, and the fur color is reddish-brown or gray.

California leaf-nosed bats have large ears, a flap of flesh on the nose (called a nose leaf), and the tail is enclosed by membrane. They are tan, gray, or light brown and a lighter color below.

Townsend's big-eared bats have large ears, two lumps (these are glands) on the side of the muzzle, and the tail does not extend beyond the tail membrane. The fur color is brown or gray with lighter underparts.

Lesser long-nosed bats have a long muzzle and a "leafed" nose. No tail is visible. They are tan or gray.

Mexican long-tongued bats have long muzzles with a "leafed" nose. They are gray or brown, and they also have a small tail.

Size and Weight:

Bat Species and Measurements	Total Length (Inches)	Tail (Inches)	Ear (Inches)	Forearm (Inches)	Weight (Ounces)
Big free-tailed bat	5	2.1	1.1	2.26–2.50	1.2
California leaf-nosed bat	3.8	1.3	1.3	1.87–2.10	0.4
Townsend's big-eared bat	3.9	1.8	1.4	1.56–1.75	0.4
Lesser long-nosed bat	3	No tail	0.6	1.99–2.18	0.6
Mexican long-tongued bat	3.5	1.6	0.7	1.68–1.87	0.6

Average Lifespan: Bats can live 10–30 years, depending on the species.

Diet: The lesser long-nosed bat and Mexican long-tongued bat both feed on nectar, pollen, and fruit. The big free-tailed, California leaf-nosed, and Townsend's big-eared bats are insectivorous and forage for flying insects, as well as those found on the ground.

California leaf-nosed bat

Townsend's big-eared bat

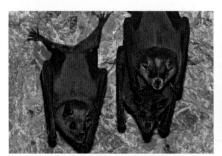

Lesser long-nosed bat

Mexican long-tongued bat

Reproduction: Nectar bats breed in early spring, and the young are born in May. Lesser long-nosed bats form large maternal colonies to raise their young, but Mexican long-tongued bats form much smaller colonies. Townsend's big-eared bats breed in the winter and females store sperm for later ovulation, which occurs in late winter or early spring. One pup is then born in summer. Big free-tailed bats also have their young during summer. California leaf-nosed bats mate in the fall and fertilization takes place immediately, but embryo growth is delayed until spring, and a single pup is born in the summer. Once born, young grow quickly and can fly within 4 weeks.

Predators: Snakes, owls, bobcats, coyote, and raptors prey on these bats.

When to Look: Bats are nocturnal and forage at night. Nectar bats forage on columnar cacti and agaves, and these plants are a good place to look for nectar bats. Insectivorous bats hunt for insects and are often seen around outdoor lights and sources of water.

Most Threatening Factor: Humans kill bats by destroying their roosts, poisoning them with pesticides, and destroying habitat.

Coping with Desert Life: Bats are nocturnal and sleep in roosts, which are found in cool areas such as rock crevices, human structures, caves, mines, or tree cavities. Foraging at night helps them stay cool and conserve moisture.

Notes: A single bat can capture hundreds of mosquitoes in one hour! The 15 million Mexican free-tailed bats at the Bracken Cave in Texas consume 250 tons of insects nightly, and many bat species eat a third or even half of their body weight in insects each night. Bats are important for plants too. Desert ecosystems in Arizona depend on nectar-feeding bats, which pollinate many columnar cacti and agaves. Many desert animals forage on the fruit and flowers of these plants.

In the roost, bats hang upside down, but have you ever wondered why? They do this for several reasons. Some bats are large, so hanging upside down on the roof of a cave, mine, or other surface allows them to take flight quickly, as all they have to do is drop down and fly off! In addition, a bat's wings are fragile and hanging upside down protects them. Perhaps the best reason is simple: safety! Predators can't reach them in their roosts, and being upside down doesn't bother bats, as they've adapted to it. Incredibly, when a mother bat is out foraging, "auntie" bats often stay with the young in the roost to protect them.

White-throated woodrat

Rats, Mice, and Shrews

(White-throated woodrat, Merriam's kangaroo rat, Southern grasshopper mouse, Desert pocket mouse, Desert shrew)

Distinguishing Features: White-throated woodrats (woodrat, packrat, trade rat) are large rats with tan fur above and white below. The throat is white. The ears are large and the tail is thick with short hairs. The eyes are huge and darkly colored.

Merriam's kangaroo rat is the smallest kangaroo rat in the U.S. It is buff, tan, or cinnamon in color and white below. The hind legs are long and the front legs are small. The long tail is bushy at the tip with brown on top and white below. The thighs are whitish.

Southern grasshopper mice have light brown to pale cinnamon in color on the back and white below. The body is round and stout. The legs are short, and the tail is thick, short, and has a white tip.

Desert pocket mice are medium-size with yellow-brown or yellow-gray fur on the back with white underparts. The tail is long, fluffed at the end, and brown above and white below.

Deer mice are medium-size. The fur on the back is pale gray mixed with red brown; the underparts are white. The tail is lightly ringed in black and white; the naked ears and eyes are large.

Desert shrews are gray-brown above and light gray below. The short tail is gray above and white below. This is the only shrew in the deserts of the Southwest.

Size and Weight:

Species and Measurements	Total Length (Inches)	Tail (Inches)	Weight (Ounces)
White-throated woodrat	11–16	3–7	5–10
Merriam's kangaroo rat	7.6–11	4.7–7	1.1–1.9
Southern grasshopper mouse	5–6	1.6–2.3	0.7–1.4
Desert pocket mouse	6–7	3.2–4.3	0.45–.70
Deer mouse	5–8.8	2–5	0.35–1.0
Desert shrew	3–3.8	0.9–1.2	0.1–.21

Merriam's kangaroo rat

Southern grasshopper mouse

Desert pocket mouse

Deer mouse

Desert shrew

Average Lifespan: Most rodents only live for weeks to months, for several years at the most.

Diet: Rats eat seeds, grasses, and some green vegetation. Woodrats also eat spiny cacti, yucca pods, nuts, and berries. Deer and desert pocket mice eat seeds, nuts, berries, fruit, insects, and green vegetation. The deer mouse will also eat some animal material. Southern grasshopper mice are carnivorous predators that eat scorpions, beetles, grasshoppers, centipedes, small mice, lizards, insects, seeds, and grass. Desert shrews eat worms, crickets, cockroaches, sow bugs, centipedes, moths, beetles, spiders, lizards, and carrion.

Reproduction: Most of these rodents can breed at almost any time of year, but most reproduction coincides with the season in which the most food is available (summer months and rainfall). They have 2–4 litters per year and 1-8 young are born in each litter. All young are hairless, blind, and dependent on the adult at birth. The young mature rapidly and are usually on their own by 30–40 days.

Predators: Almost all carnivores (bobcats, coyotes, badgers, and foxes) eat rodents, as do snakes, hawks, owls, and Gila monsters.

When to Look: All of these rodents are nocturnal, but some may also be crepuscular (active in the early morning and late afternoon). Some rodents frequent campgrounds and human habitations.

Most Threatening Factor: Prolonged periods of drought or floods can be detrimental to rodents. Drought can cause them to starve, and floods can drown rodents in their burrows.

Coping with Desert Life: Southern grasshopper mice are one of the fiercest and most voracious predators out there! Don't let their small size fool you; they are a wolf in a mouse's clothing. They kill other mice with a swift bite to the neck (just as mountain lions kill their prey), and when preying upon a scorpion, they quickly bite off its stinger in order to eat the disarmed animal. They also sometimes allow scorpions to sting them repeatedly, as they're largely immune to the toxin and it simply causes them to go somewhat numb, allowing them to consume the scorpion without further trouble. They have a different strategy for pinacate beetles, which emit a foul substance from a gland on their hindquarters when threatened. Grasshopper mice stuff the beetle's butt into the ground and then proceed to eat the beetle. What's more, grasshopper mice are well known for howling. They stand on hind feet, throw the head back, and emit a loud sound like a howl! The howl is used to communicate, and the sound can travel quite far in the desert air.

Rock squirrel

Squirrels

(Rock squirrel, White-tailed antelope squirrel)

Distinguishing Features: Rock squirrels are large squirrels with mottled grayish-brown fur, small ears, and a long bushy tail. Their underparts are white.

White-tailed antelope squirrels have grayish-brown to cinnamon fur on the back, white underparts, and a short tail that is dark on the top and lighter on the bottom. They also have a white stripe on the sides running from the shoulder to the rump. This squirrel has noticeable cheek pouches.

Size and Weight: Rock squirrels are 19 inches long with an 8-inch tail. They weigh 1.7 pounds. They are the largest of the desert ground squirrels.

White-tailed antelope squirrels are 5–7 inches long, excluding the tail, which is 2–3.7 inches long. They weigh 4–5 ounces.

Average Lifespan: Rock squirrels can live 6–10 years in the wild and longer in captivity. White-tailed antelope squirrels usually only live 1–2 years in the wild, but they can live up to 6 years in captivity.

Diet: Squirrels eat fruits, seeds, plant stems, flower blooms, berries, bulbs, roots, insects (beetles, ants, crickets, grasshoppers), lizards, and carrion. Rock squirrels will also eat small rodents, birds, and bird eggs.

Reproduction: Rock squirrels give birth to young during the spring. Gestation lasts 23–31 days, and 5–8 young are born on average. They may have a second litter in the same year. White-tailed antelope squirrels breed February–June. Their gestation takes about 30–35 days and there is usually only one litter per year, and it produces anywhere from 5–14 young.

Predators: Many carnivores and omnivores feed on squirrels. The list includes coyotes, bobcats, foxes, ringtails, and coatis, as well as snakes, roadrunners, and birds of prey.

When to Look: Both of these squirrels are diurnal and easily seen. They can be observed around campgrounds, human buildings, and regularly climb vegetation, cactus, or rocks for food or a better view.

White-tailed antelope squirrel

Most Threatening Factor: Humans kill squirrels with poison and traps.

Coping with Desert Life: White-tailed antelope squirrels are well adapted to desert life. Their body temperature can exceed 110 degrees without harming them, and when they begin to overheat, they rub saliva on the face to cool off. They also obtain much of their moisture from fruits and juicy food, and their specialized kidneys help them conserve water.

Both of these squirrels are diurnal, and they are mostly active during early morning or later in the day. They both also use burrows to stay cool.

Notes: A lot of birds and mammals don't like rattlesnakes! Rock squirrels are no exception and react very dramatically when encountering a rattler: They emit a loud, shrill high-pitched whistle and wave their large, bushy tail, which also heats up, fooling the rattlesnake's heat sensors into thinking that a much larger target is present. As they do so, the squirrels also proceed to throw dirt and small rocks at the offending snake!

Most snakes prefer not confront a belligerent squirrel and leave immediately. They do so for a good reason: In many cases, squirrels proceed to team up and "mob" the rattler, sometimes even killing and eating it. What about the rattler's venom, you ask? If a squirrel is bit, it may not be the end of the line. Many adult squirrels are somewhat immune to snake venom.

Rock squirrels are as comfortable in canyons, hillsides, and cliffs as they are in deserts. They will climb trees but spend more time on the ground. Their dens are located underground and found beneath rocks, trees, or vegetation. They choose burrows that are close to lookout points such as rocks or cliffs, as this enables them to keep an eye on things. They don't use the same den for long, either, and may use several within their home range. This likely helps them avoid predators.

Rock squirrels are colonial and share their habitat with other squirrels. But one male is dominant over the other males and carries out most of the breeding. The dominant male may even drive off the subordinate males during the breeding season. After the breeding season, some of the subordinate males may be allowed to return to the colony.

White-tailed antelope squirrels are active all year long and are very well adapted to the harsh desert climate. They never seem to slow down and are often seen during the hottest daylight hours. If antelope squirrels overheat, they cool off in their burrows and then resume their activities later. They often sit on top of Joshua trees, saguaros, or palo verde trees watching for predators; when they spot a threat, they emit a high whistle as a warning to other squirrels.

Antelope squirrels often stop in front of their underground burrow, look around, and then dive in; they don't hibernate, but several squirrels will share a burrow and huddle together for warmth during the winter.

North American porcupine

Porcupines are also adept, if somewhat slow, climbers. They don't jump when climbing or descending. Their excellent balance helps prevent falls, but if a porcupine falls, it can be pierced by its own quills. Thankfully, its quills are coated with a natural antibiotic that helps prevent infection from setting in on many occasions.

North American Porcupine

Distinguishing Features: Large rodents with special quills on the back, sides, and tail, porcupines have gray-brown bodies covered in yellow-tipped hairs. They have a brown-black face, short legs, long, curved claws, and a stocky body. Porcupines are well adapted for arboreal life (living in trees). The soles of their wide feet have fleshy knobs.

Size and Weight: From head to rump, porcupines are 18–26 inches; the tail is 7–9 inches long. Porcupines weigh 10–35 pounds, and males are larger than females.

Average Lifespan: For rodents, porcupines are long-lived. Some individuals can live 9–12 years in the wild and even longer in captivity.

Diet: Porcupines eat twigs and the inner bark of trees, as well as buds, roots, berries, flowers, seeds, fruits, herbs, green plants, and leaves.

Reproduction: Breeding occurs in September and October. Dens are located in hollow trees, logs, or in caves, underground burrows, and rock crevices. Gestation lasts about 204–215 days, and one young (called a porcupette) is usually born April–May. Young are born with their eyes wide open, sport developed teeth, and can walk unsteadily right after being born. A porcupette's quills are soft but harden within hours of birth. Young can climb trees within days, and they can eat vegetation within several weeks of birth. They are on their own before the end of the year.

Predators: Mountain lions, bobcats, coyotes, common ravens, and great horned owls prey on porcupines.

When to Look: Porcupines are mostly nocturnal, but you may observe them resting in trees. They are also observed along roads.

Most Threatening Factors: Porcupines are fond of salt and can be found often around roads and highways, where many are killed by traffic. Because porcupines crave salt (a consequence of a low-sodium diet), they are also often found gnawing on a variety of wooden structures and implements that contain salt (either from wood treatments or contact with human perspiration), including cabins, ax handles, paddles, and even outhouses. Humans also kill porcupines for quills.

Coping with Desert Life: Porcupines are mainly nocturnal; they are active during the evening.

Notes: Porcupines are most famous for their quills (30,000 of them!), but contrary to myth, they don't actually throw their quills at attackers. Instead, they raise their quills up, often turning their back to the threat. Each quill is needle-sharp (up to 3 inches long) and has hundreds of tiny backwards-facing barbs. They don't come out easily. In fact, the barbs actually cause the quill to work its way further into the skin, at rates of 1 millimeter or more per hour! If infection or organ damage results, quills can kill the offender over time.

Porcupines are usually in no hurry and waddle along on the ground; after all, they carry their own arsenal to protect themselves from predators! Their eyesight is poor, but their senses of smell and hearing are excellent. To communicate, porcupines produce grunts, snorts, whines, screams, barks, teeth clicking, and screeches. Low frequency sounds are common.

Porcupines are lethargic and sedentary most of the time, but during the breeding season the males become active and aggressive. Both males and females leave urine signals, which are "read" by other porcupines at dens, on trees, and along trails. Courtship is vocal and the males locate the females by smell. Males will aggressively fight other males for the opportunity to breed with the females. Courtship includes a comical dance, and right before mating, the male sprays the female with urine. After mating, the female has nothing to do with the male and raises the young without any assistance.

Porcupettes are born with very soft quills; the quills don't harm the mother during the birth. But the quills harden within a few hours after birth. Porcupettes play by striking with their tails, lifting the quills, and backing up into objects, which is what the adults do when threatened.

What do porcupine tracks and scat look like? Porcupine tracks are about 2.5–3.5 inches long and 1.5 inches wide. The track is oval with large heel pads; there are 5 small toes on the hind feet and 4 on the front feet, and long claws. The toes are pointed inward. The porcupine has a short stride, and they waddle when walking. Prints are found about 5–6 inches apart. The soles of the feet are unique, with fleshy knobs. Porcupines sweep the tail back and forth when walking, and this behavior may make a path look as if the dirt has been swept aside. Porcupine scat is pellet-sized and 0.75 to 1 inch long and 0.37 inch in diameter. It's also oblong, and yellow in color, and a group of pellets are usually found. Look for pellets at the base of trees, caves, mines, hollow logs, or near underground burrows.

In the past, many states offered bounties on porcupines because of the damage porcupines cause to seedlings, mature plants, wooden houses and structures, and vehicle tires (because of the presence of road salt), but today local control measures usually work well.

Porcupines can carry a few parasites, such as ticks, fleas, mites, lice, tapeworms, and nematodes. Nonetheless, they don't carry very many diseases that can be transmitted to humans other than tick fever and tularemia (which is transmitted to humans by dogs exposed to porcupines).

Striped skunk

Striped Skunk

Distinguishing Features: Skunks are stocky animals with a small head and ears and short legs. Its long black coat features a white stripe that starts at the head and runs down its back before splitting into a V-like shape.

Size and Weight: The head and body are 13–18 inches long; the tail is 7–15 inches long. Skunks weigh 7–15 pounds.

Average Lifespan: Skunks live 2–3 years in the wild and 6 years or more in captivity.

Diet: Skunks are omnivores and eat both plants and animals; they eat insects, birds and eggs, rodents, rabbits, worms, fruit, berries, and carrion.

Reproduction: When breeding, striped skunks are promiscuous and the males breed with multiple females. During the breeding season, males become very active and will cover longer distances than normal (up to 5 miles a night) in search of females.

Skunks breed in February–March and gestation lasts 60–70 days; because of delayed implantation, fertilized eggs aren't immediately implanted in the female. Around 5–6 blind and helpless young (kits) are born in April–May. The kits' eyes open in 3 weeks and the young will follow the mother (single file) within several months on foraging trips. Females care for the young; males do not, and can even pose a threat, as they will even eat the young if the opportunity arises. Kits may hang around with the female for months after birth and even after they can forage on their own.

Predators: Coyotes, bobcats, and great horned owls and other raptors.

When to Look: Skunks are nocturnal and are often seen around camp-sites, garbage cans, and human dwellings. Skunks are usually not afraid of humans.

Most Threatening Factors: Humans are the greatest threat to skunks. The fur is valuable to humans, though it's usually dyed and labeled as "American sable" instead of skunk fur. Many skunks are also killed by vehicles, and skunks also fall victim to disease (especially rabies, pneumonia, distemper, and leptospirosis).

Coping with Desert Life: Skunks are nocturnal and avoid the heat of the day by roosting in burrows, wood and rock piles, and hollow logs.

Notes: When threatened, skunks stomp the ground with their front feet, raise the tail, and even charge in warning. But if this display doesn't deter an attacker, they move to the launch sequence! The skunk's spray (musk) can be expelled for 13 feet or more and they can spray again immediately if necessary. When spraying, skunks contract the muscles around two glands that are found near the base of their tail, and the musk is sprayed in small droplets or as a stream. The musk is made up of sulfur compounds; aside from the awful smell, it's deadly if ingested and very painful if it enters the eyes. The odor is offensive and revolting and very difficult to remove from clothes, hair, skin, and fur. Kits as young as eight days old can emit the musk, even though they don't at all at that age. The moral of this story is clear: Give skunks the right of way!

Skunks are gregarious and may share dens with other skunks. Usually only one male shares the communal underground den with numerous females. Skunks don't hibernate in the winter but may become inactive during periods of cold weather. Before the cold weather arrives, skunks eat constantly and put on a thick layer of fat for the winter. They may lose up to 15–30 percent of their body weight during this time.

Skunks may dig their own burrows or they may use an abandoned animal burrow, such as one created by a fox, badger, squirrel, or gopher. If the temperature warms enough on a winter's day, the skunk will wake and actively seek food.

During the summer, many skunk burrows are found aboveground, and can be found in rock piles, crevices, in thick vegetation, mesquite thickets, or in hollow logs. Striped skunks are not territorial, and the home ranges of many individual skunks overlap.

Skunks get their foul-smelling spray from a pair of scent glands on their rump; in captive animals, these glands can be removed, but this makes the skunk defenseless against dogs and other predators. (In the early 1900s, skunks were raised in captivity for their fur.) Nonetheless, skunks can contract rabies, and rabid skunks are very aggressive, so attempting to "domesticate" a skunk isn't recommended. In most states it is illegal to own a skunk as a pet.

Skunks have well-developed front claws that they use to dig up insects and other small animals that live under logs, rocks, branches, and litter. Skunks often spend the night flipping over rocks and other debris while looking for food. Their fondness for eating grasshoppers, grubs, agriculture pests, and rodents helps farmers.

Skunks can be nuisances around campgrounds. Unattended food on picnic tables is fair game, and skunks often climb inside of garbage cans in search of an easy meal. When discovered, they don't seem to be bothered by humans, and attempting to scare them off may provoke a spraying attack! They are also comfortable around houses and will often sleep under structures, such as porches.

A striped skunk's tracks show 5 toes with claw marks on each pad. The toe pads are elongated; the front tracks are 1 inch long and 1 inch wide. The hind track is 1.5 inches long and 1 inch wide. The heel pad is large and divided into 2 parts. The scat is 1.5–2 inches long and 0.5 inch in diameter; the scat is oblong, medium-size, and blunt on the ends.

Many bird species are very comfortable in deserts, and the deserts of the Southwest are no exception. They are home to a wide variety of species, from the iconic roadrunner and the massive golden eagle to the turkey vulture and the tiny burrowing owl.

Some of our desert birds are year-long residents, while others come to the area to nest in the summer or migrate through. Surviving in the arid and deadly environment of a desert is difficult enough, but the birds of the Southwest not only survive, they somehow manage to thrive, making them some of the easiest denizens of the deserts to spot.

Red-tailed hawk

Raptors

(Hawks, Falcons, Eagles, Vultures)

Distinguishing Features: Red-tailed hawks (Harlan's hawk, western red-tailed hawk) have broad wings that are two-toned on the underside; a dark brown body; and a short, broad, bright-red tail. The body is stocky with a dark belly band on its rust-colored breast.

Cooper's hawks (chicken hawk, quail hawk, big blue darter) have a gray back, streaked rust-colored underparts, and a long rudder-like tail that is barred and gray-black. The tip of the tail is white, and the legs are yellow. They hold their wings straight when flying.

Ferruginous hawks (ferruginous rough-leg) are brown or reddish above, with a white breast, neck, and tail, and feet covered in red or brown feathers. They soar with slightly upturned wings.

Swainson's hawks (grasshopper hawk, brown hawk) are brown on the back and on the back of the head, with a white or light-colored breast. They are rust-colored on the neck and upper breast, and have a white face. The underside of the long, pointed wings is two-toned (light and gray color). A dark morph occurs occasionally.

American kestrels (American sparrow hawk, desert sparrow hawk, little kestrel) have reddish bars on the back and on the underparts. The head has a black, white, and gray pattern. The wings and tail are long and pointed. The male has blue-gray wings. The breast is streaked with rust.

Golden eagles (black eagle, brown eagle, Calumet eagle, royal eagle) are dark brown and buff-to-golden-colored on the head and under the tail. The tail is grayish black and two-toned. The broad, long wings are slightly tilted upward when soaring.

Turkey vultures (scavengers, buzzards) are dark with long, two-toned wings that tilt slightly upward when soaring. The tail is long and gray and the legs have no feathers. The body color is black and the small naked head is bright red.

Size and Weight: The Red-tailed, Swainson's, and ferruginous hawks are all medium-size. Ferruginous hawks are heaviest at 3.5 pounds on average, followed by red-tailed hawks (2.4 pounds) and Swainson's (1.9 pounds). They all have short, broad wings. The golden eagle is a large bird and weighs around 10 pounds. The American kestrel is our smallest falcon and only weighs about 4 ounces. The Cooper's hawk weighs about 1 pound. The turkey vulture is one of three vulture species (black vulture, California condor) that live in the Southwest, and it weighs about 4 pounds.

Cooper's hawk

Ferruginous hawk

Swainson's hawk

American kestrel

Golden eagle

Turkey vulture

Average Lifespan: Most raptors live about 5–6 years or longer. Eagles can live into their twenties.

Diet: All raptors are carnivores. The red-tailed, Swainson's, and ferruginous hawks eat rodents, rabbits, snakes, and lizards, as does the golden eagle. Swainson's hawks also eat insects. American kestrels eat insects and small rodents. The Cooper's hawk specializes in small birds, mammals, and lizards. Turkey vultures are the garbage disposals of the desert and eat carrion. Some hawks and eagles also eat carrion.

Reproduction: Birds of prey nest in spring and summer. Most use trees, cliffs, telephone poles, and other man-made structures for nests. American kestrels use tree cavities or those found in cacti. Turkey vultures nest on the ground, in caves, in boulder piles, and in other sheltered locations. Many birds of prey mate for life and both the male and female care for the young. Most raptors lay

3–6 eggs (vultures lay 1–3), and the nestling period is 25–37 days (72–84 days for eagles). Usually only 1–4 nestlings survive to leave the nest. Many nestlings take 30 days or longer to fledge (develop feathers). Fledglings remain dependent on the parents for several weeks or more after fledging (up to 11 weeks or more for eagles). If the first clutch is lost, some raptors lay a second clutch.

Predators: Carnivorous predators like coyotes, bobcats, foxes, and badgers feed on birds of prey, if they can capture them. Nestlings are taken by other birds, carnivores, and snakes.

When to Look: All of these raptors can be seen during the day. They may be resting in trees or bushes during the heat of the day, or soaring above while they look for food.

Most Threatening Factors: Migratory raptors face huge dangers during migration and once they reach their wintering grounds. Humans shoot and trap raptors, and habitat destruction is another real threat. Raptors are also threatened by "downstream" pollution that they ingest when they eat carrion killed with lead shot.

Coping with Desert Life: Feathers help protect raptors from the worst of cold weather and heat. As birds are also mobile, they have more-ready access to water, and often cool off as you'd suspect, with baths, or by resting in the shade.

Notes: Vultures cool off via "urohidrosis." When the vulture is hot, it urinates on its legs and as the moisture evaporates, it cools the blood underneath the skin of the legs. As the cooled blood circulates, the bird cools! In fact, vultures usually have a white coating on their legs, and that's the source. But vultures aren't especially dirty; the remaining uric acid is removed when they bathe.

Common barn owl

Owls

(Great horned owl, Common barn owl, Burrowing owl)

Distinguishing Features: Great horned owls (Western great horned owl) are a mottled gray on the back, barred gray and white on the underside, and they have large ear tufts and a dish-shaped face. The eyes are yellow. Both sexes look similar.

Common barn owls (golden owl, monkey-faced owl) are golden-brown above with gray spots and flecks. They have white underparts with gray spots, a heart-shaped white face, and black eyes. The legs are long, and the tail is short. Females are slightly darker than the males.

Burrowing owls (Billy owl, prairie dog owl, Western burrowing owl) are brown with light spots above and streaks below, a white throat and eyebrows, and long legs. The eyes are yellow. Both sexes look similar.

Size and Weight: Great horned owls are large and weigh 3 pounds. Common barn owls are medium-size and weigh 1 pound. Burrowing owls are tiny and weigh just 5 ounces.

Average Lifespan: Owls live about 4–15 years in the wild but longer in captivity.

Diet: All these owls are carnivorous and prey on small mammals (rodents, rabbits, skunks, and bats), as well as birds and insects. Burrowing owls also prey on scorpions and beetles.

Reproduction: Great horned owls and barn owls nest in trees, caves, mines, on cliff faces or rock outcrops, in stumps, and in manmade structures. Burrowing owls reside in the burrows of rodents and other mammals. Owl breeding occurs in the spring or summer. The female lays 2–9 eggs, and incubation lasts 26–35 days. Females do most of the incubation, and males bring food to the nest for the female. Owlets fledge (develop wing feathers) at 32–62 days and are cared for by the parents for weeks to months after fledging. Even so, mortality is high for the owlets.

Predators: Great horned owls will prey on barn owls. Snakes, foxes, coyotes, badgers, raccoons, and raptors can kill burrowing owls and barn owls. Sadly, humans are predators of owls too.

Great horned owl

Burrowing owl

When to Look: Great horned owls and common barn owls are nocturnal and secretive. But listening for their hoot or screech call may disclose their location. Burrowing owls are active both day and night; to find them, look for the mounds that these small owls use as roosts and lookout perches.

Most Threatening Factors: Agricultural practices have negatively impacted common barn owls, and all too often great horned owls are shot, hit by cars, or are impacted by habitat destruction. Rodent poisoning, insecticide use, and the conversion of rangelands to agriculture have caused burrowing owl numbers to fall in the West. Burrowing owls thrive in traditional rangelands and areas with open and dry vegetation. They prefer habitat amid low grasslands, desert vegetation, or heavily grazed land. A study carried out in California indicated that common barn owls avoided areas of little vegetation, and barn owl populations have disappeared in intensely cultivated areas.

Coping with Desert Life: Most owls are nocturnal and avoid the day-time heat by roosting in vegetation, caves, mines, and human-made structures. Burrowing owls roost underground in cool shelters. Birds can also pant, which helps dissipate heat, by opening their bills. They obtain water from their food.

Notes: Owls are silent hunters! Modifications to the first primary feather of the wing enable owls to fly silently and sneak up on prey. Other birds have smooth flight feathers and the air passing over this area produces sound. In owls, the outer edge of the flight feather is serrated; this disrupts airflow and ensures silent flight. So before a rodent realizes that an owl is nearby, the owl has pounced and the rodent is a goner!

Owls also have other adaptations that improve their hearing. Common barn owls have a heart-shaped facial mask that helps channel sound to the ears. Barn owls have very sensitive hearing, in large part because of the stiff feathers on the face. These feathers function as a reflector and guide sound into the ears.

Once the owl hears potential prey, it turns towards the sound and uses its hearing to accurately locate a target's position. It can do so because an owl's ears are located at different heights on its head, enabling it to pinpoint sound on both the vertical and the horizontal planes. This helps an owl accurately gauge the distance of a target. Barn owls are a perfect example: They pounce on prey with amazing accuracy, even in total darkness.

Greater roadrunner

BELIEVE IT OR NOT

Most animals avoid rattlesnakes, but road-runners actually seek them out—in order to eat them! Bird pairs usually act together to subdue a snake. While one bird approaches the snake from the front, the other bird sneaks up behind it, grabs it, and crushes its head on a rock or the ground.

Other Notable Birds

(Greater roadrunner, Black-chinned hummingbird, Northern mockingbird, White-winged dove, Black-throated sparrow, Say's phoebe)

Distinguishing Features: Greater roadrunners have a long tail and brown-cream streaks on the back and lighter-colored underparts. The bill is long and there is a colorful blue-red streak behind the eye. The crest on the head is often raised. Both sexes look alike.

Black-chinned hummingbirds have a green back, a white collar, a black chin with a thin purple band, and a long bill. Their underparts are a mottled gray, and they have a white spot behind the eye and the wings are dark. Females lack the black chin and purple band.

Northern mockingbirds have a gray back, white underparts, and a dark eyeline. They also have white patches on the wing, a short bill, and a long black-and-white tail. Both sexes look similar.

White-winged doves look similar to pigeons but are brown in color, with a white streak on dark wings and a dark tail with a white tip. Their legs are orange, and they have a black spot on the cheek. Both sexes look similar.

Black-throated sparrows have a light brownish-gray back, lighter underparts, a black throat and upper breast, and a black-and-white head pattern. The tail is dark, with white tips on the corners; these sparrows also have a white eyebrow. Both sexes look similar.

Say's phoebes have a gray back, head, and wings. The tail is long and black and the belly is light red. The face also has a dark eye line. Both sexes look alike.

Size and Weight: Roadrunners are large and weigh 13 ounces. Black-chinned hummingbirds are very small and weigh just 0.12 ounce. Mockingbirds are medium-size and weigh 1.7 ounces. White-winged doves are medium-size and weigh 5 ounces. Black-throated sparrows are also tiny, weighing just 0.47 ounce. Say's phoebes weigh only 0.74 ounce.

Average Lifespan: Most birds live 3–4 years; mortality is high in the first year of life.

Diet: Hummingbirds drink nectar from flowers and also eat small insects. Say's phoebes and mockingbirds eat insects and berries. Doves eat seeds and cactus fruit. Black-throated sparrows feed on seeds, plants, and insects. Roadrunners eat small mammals, birds, lizards, snakes, scorpions, insects, cactus fruits, and seeds.

Black-chinned hummingbird

Northern mockingbird

White-winged dove

Black-throated sparrow

Say's phoebe

Reproduction: Scrubs, trees, and cactus are used for nests. All of these species form pair bonds, except for hummingbirds. Breeding and nesting occurs in the spring and summer. Hummingbirds lay 1–2 eggs. Roadrunners, mockingbirds, white-winged doves, black-throated sparrows and Say's phoebes lay 1–6 eggs. Incubation lasts 13–20 days and nestlings fledge after 11–18 days. All nestlings are altricial (blind and naked) and dependent on parents. Bird pairs can produce a second clutch if the first fails.

Predators: Raptors, carnivorous mammals, snakes, and humans. Roadrunners sometimes kill hummingbirds.

When to Look: Birds are often found near water sources; all of the birds discussed here are diurnal and active throughout the day, except when it is very hot. Hummingbirds can often be seen at nectar flowers or preying upon insects. Say's phoebes feed on insects too.

Most Threatening Factors: Shooting, trapping, pesticides, and loss of crucial habitat all threaten these birds.

Coping with Desert Life: Birds that eat insects, animals, and fruits obtain moisture from their diet, and birds avoid the worst of the heat by resting in the shade and limiting activity to early morning or late afternoon.

Notes: Male and female white-winged doves produce a "milk" that they feed to nestlings. The curd-like fluid is secreted from cells in the crop, a specialized pouch found in adult birds. The milk is very nutritious and contains more protein and fat than cow's milk or human milk. It's the only food that the nestlings have for at least the first two weeks after they hatch, and the young grow quickly on this rich milk!

Roadrunners prefer hunting rattlesnakes in tandem with another roadrunner, but they'll hunt alone too. If the roadrunner is alone, it will tease and harass the snake until it tires and then go in for the kill. It then eats as much of the snake as possible, sometimes leaving the rest of the uneaten snake hanging out of its mouth as the rest is slowly digested.

When hummingbirds aren't able to obtain the 10–12 calories daily they need to survive—an immense total compared to their weight— they can slip into a state known as torpor. When this occurs, the heartbeat and breathing slow, and the body temperature drops significantly. Torpor helps a hummingbird conserve almost 30 percent of its energy. A small body size enables a hummingbird to take advantage of this energy-saving adaptation!

Snakes are among the most famous—and feared—inhabitants found in our Southwestern deserts. Nonetheless, the vast majority of the snakes found here pose little to no risk to people. Exceptions include the rattlesnake and the coral snake, which pack a venom potent enough to pose a medical emergency. Thankfully, snakebites are quite rare, as snakes almost always prefer to flee.

The desert is also home to a wide variety of lizards, from the colorful (and venomous) Gila monster to the lesser-known but far more common zebra-tailed lizards, which are often seen darting from place to place throughout the desert.

Western rattlesnake

Venomous Snakes

(Western rattlesnake, Western diamondback rattlesnake, Mojave rattlesnake, Western coral snake)

Distinguishing Features: Western rattlesnakes (prairie or Hopi rattlesnakes) are brown to dark brown with lighter blotches. They have a light-colored line that runs from the back of the eye to the edge of the mouth, dark and light rings on the tail, and a triangle or diamond-shaped head. Their belly ranges from light to dark brown. Western rattlesnakes are the most widely distributed rattlesnake in the Southwest.

Western diamondback rattlesnakes (adobe snake, Arizona diamond rattlesnake, coon tail) have dark, diamond-shaped blotches on the back, a light-colored line that runs from the back of the eye to the edge of the mouth, and tail bands ranging from black and ash-white to pale gray. The head is triangle-shaped, and the belly is off-white.

Mojave rattlesnakes (Mojave green) have diamond-shaped blotches that range from brown to green and green to light gray. The scales are light-colored. A whitish-yellow stripe runs from the back of the eye to the mouth, there are narrow black-and-white bands on the tail, and the head is triangle-shaped. The scales on the snout are large. The snake's underparts are green-gray to yellow.

Western coral snakes (Arizona and Sonoran coral snake) have broad red, black, and white or yellow bands. There are paler bands on the underparts and head and tail are black.

Size and Weight: Western rattlesnakes are 15–65 inches long. The Western diamondback rattlesnake is the largest Western rattlesnake, ranging from 30–84 inches. The Mojave rattlesnake is 24–51 inches long and has the most potent venom of all the rattlesnakes in our region. Western coral snakes are slender and are 13–30 inches long.

Average Lifespan: Rattlesnakes can live 20–25 years in captivity but less than that in the wild.

Diet: Rattlesnakes are carnivorous and eat rabbits, rodents, birds, lizards, and eggs. Coral snakes eat other snakes and lizards.

Reproduction: Rattlesnakes are usually sexually mature by the age of 3. Males fight each other over females. Many males exhibit a behavior called "topping" in which they wrap their body around the vertical body of an opponent, forcing the other snake downward. Rattlesnakes give birth to live young in summer. Coral snakes lay eggs in

Western diamondback rattlesnake

Mojave rattlesnake

Western coral snake

late summer. Rattlesnakes have 2–25 young and the young disperse almost immediately, receiving no parental care.

Predators: Raptors, roadrunners, coyotes, bobcats, foxes, badgers, and humans threaten snakes.

When to Look: Most rattlesnakes are nocturnal, but they can also be active in the early morning or later in the day. Early evening is a good time to observe snakes. The coral snake is very secretive and difficult to observe.

Most Threatening Factor: Snakes are persecuted by humans, and many snakes are killed each year. Snakes are killed in organized "snake hunts" where they are shot, trapped, or poisoned. Many others are hit by cars, and snake habitat is destroyed by agriculture and development.

Coping with Desert Life: During the heat of the day, snakes seek the shade and comfort offered by rodent burrows, shrubs, caves, mines, crevices or rock piles.

Notes: Rattlesnakes are known as "pit vipers" because they have special heat-sensing pits on the face that are located between the eyes and the nostrils. These depressions are essentially temperature sensors that tell a snake when prey is close by; given that rattlesnakes feed on a variety of small warm-blooded mammals, this is essential information. What's more, these pits can help a snake determine the size of nearby prey, even in total darkness!

Rattlesnake rattles are made up of hollow segments of keratin, the same material that makes up fingernails and hair. A rattlesnake vibrates its tail as a defensive or warning mechanism. New segments of the rattle are added after each molting cycle.

When a rattlesnake bites its victim, it transfers venom from two glands into its hypodermic fangs, which can be up to an inch long. The fangs are normally folded up and are out of the way when not in use. Rattlesnake venom is complex and can cause severe tissue damage and even death. The victim experiences severe pain, swelling, chills, weakness, numbness, nausea, and bleeding. Respiration may also become irregular. Thankfully, antivenin exists, and when promptly applied it can reduce and eliminate these symptoms. The best way to prevent a snakebite, venomous or not, is just to leave snakes be! If you're bitten, get to a hospital as soon as possible. Do not administer drugs, a tourniquet, apply ice, or use any other first aid.

Gopher snake

BELIEVE IT OR NOT

Snakes kill and consume many mice and rats. This fact alone makes snakes very beneficial; none-theless, many snakes are indiscriminately killed by people each year.

Other Snakes

(Nightsnake, Coachwhip, Western shovel-nosed snake, Sonoran whipsnake, Gopher snake, Long-nosed snake)

Distinguishing Features: Nightsnakes are light brown or gray with dark brown blotches on the back and sides, two dark blotches on the neck, and dark brown streaks behind the eyes. The underparts are light-colored. The head is triangle-shaped. A mild venom is used to subdue prey.

Coachwhips can be red, pink, tan, or black, and there are no horizontal stripes on the body. The underparts are lighter. Coachwhips move very fast.

Western shovel-nosed snakes have brown or black bands on a light-colored (white or yellow) body. They have a flat, shovel-shaped nose.

Sonoran whipsnakes have a blue-gray, green, or gray-brown body with lighter underparts. There are 2–3 light-colored stripes on each side of the body.

Gopher snakes are creamy-yellow in color and have dark blotches on the body and lighter underparts. The blotches are larger on the back and smaller on the sides. A dark stripe runs from the eye to the jaw.

Long-nosed snakes have black bands with white speckles and red bands with black speckles. The bands are separated by thin cream-colored stripes. The underparts are light-colored with some black spots on the sides. The edges of the bands are ragged. The nose is long and pointed.

Size and Weight: Nightsnakes are small, just 12–26 inches long. Coachwhips are long, slender snakes that are 36–102 inches long. Western shovel-nosed snakes range 10–17 inches long. Sonoran whipsnakes are 24–67 inches long. Gopher snakes can range 36–110 inches long. Long-nosed snakes are slim and just 20–41 inches long.

Average Lifespan: Most snakes live 4–5 years, but they live much longer in captivity.

Diet: Coachwhips, gopher snakes, and long-nosed snakes eat small mammals, birds, eggs, lizards, snakes, insects, and rabbits. Nightsnakes eat blind snakes (tiny subterranean snakes), frogs, and lizards. Western shovel-nosed snakes eat insects, spiders, scorpions, centipedes, and moth pupae. Sonoran whipsnakes eat birds, lizards, and frogs. Snakes consume their prey dead or alive.

Reproduction: Males engage in courtship fights, and the victor breeds with the female. The fights are usually about strength and power

Nightsnake

Coachwhip

Western shovel-nosed snake

Sonoran whipsnake

Long-nosed snake

and don't involve biting. All of these snakes lay eggs during the summer. They lay anywhere from 2 to 24 eggs.

Predators: Raptors, coyotes, bobcats, foxes, badgers, and humans prey on snakes.

When to Look: Coachwhips, gopher snakes, and long-nosed snakes can be observed during the day if temperatures are not too excessive. Coachwhips appear to prefer the hot, dry deserts more than most other snakes and may be seen out and about in daylight. Nightsnakes are difficult to observe and usually hide under rocks or vegetation. Sonoran whipsnakes are good climbers and may be seen in shrubs and cactus. Western shovel-nosed snakes prefer washes, sandy areas, and rocky habitat and are rarely seen aboveground.

Most Threatening Factors: Human predation (often because they are mistaken for potentially dangerous snakes) and human development are the greatest threats to these snakes.

Coping with Desert Life: Coachwhips and gopher snakes seem to do very well in the desert and can be observed in both the day and night. But most snakes seek shade and cool burrows during the heat of the day. The Western shovel-nosed snake burrows under sand and usually don't emerge until night. Many snakes become dormant during the winter.

Notes: The gopher snake can do a great imitation of a rattlesnake! When threatened, it hisses loudly and shakes its tail vigorously, which is exactly what a rattlesnake would do! Long-nosed snakes take this defense a little further. They can vibrate the tail too but also release blood and feces, which is more than enough to convince most critters to stay away.

Nightsnakes subdue prey (snakes, lizards, frogs) with their mild venom, which they inject via the grooved teeth at the back of the upper jaw. This venom is harmless to humans—similar to an insect bite—but it's very effective on their prey.

Western shovel-nosed snakes "swim" in the sand! Their smooth scales, flat, shovel-shaped nose, and adaptations to their lower jaw and abdomen allow them to move very quickly through the sand.

Coachwhips (also called racers) can have an unpredictable temperament and will on occasion lunge, bite, or aggressively chase you if threatened. These snakes are also very quick and are best left alone.

Sonoran collared lizard

Lizards

(Gila monster, Desert horned lizard, Desert spiny lizard, Mojave fringe-toed lizard, Sonoran collared lizard, Zebra-tailed lizard)

Distinguishing Features: Gila monsters are heavy-bodied reptiles with bead-like scales, a large head, small eyes and a thick, short tail. The body color is salmon pink with black markings. The snout and mouth area are black. The forked tongue is similar to a snake's.

Desert horned lizards are also known as horny toads, and their coloration varies with the color of the ground, so they can appear tan, beige, reddish, gray, or black. They have round, squat bodies, with a roll of fringed scales on both sides of the body, plus one roll of scales on both sides of the throat. The head has short horns or spines, and the nose is blunt. Black blotches cover the back and throat area, and the tail is fat and short.

Desert spiny lizards are light-colored (yellow, yellow-brown, or light-brown) with black markings on both sides of the neck and pointed scales. Males have a blue belly and throat and may have purple on the back.

Mojave fringe-toed lizards have a flat, whitish-gray body; they have dark spots under the tail and on the undersides. They have colored areas under the tail and on each side of body; the throat is dark. The scales are colored; adults have pink sides and a yellowish-green belly during breeding season. The sides of the toes have fringes.

Sonoran collared lizards are tan to green with light yellow bands and a large head. They have black stripes (often called collars) on the back of the neck and the long tail almost looks flat. Adult males have blue-gray throats that are black in the center. When females become pregnant they develop red spots on the sides.

Zebra-tailed lizards are also known as sand lizards, and they are lanky and slender with long legs and a long tail. They have a grayish-brown upper body and mottled spots on the back. The ears are visible and there are black and white stripes on the tail. The belly is bluish green with black bars. The rear toes are fringed.

Size and Weight: Gila monsters are large and reach 9–18 inches long. Sonoran collared lizards are a bit smaller, with a total length of 10 inches. Desert horned lizards are small, just 3–4 inches long. Desert spiny lizards are even smaller, just 2.5–5.5 inches long. Mojave fringe-toed lizards (2.75–4.5 inches long) and Zebra-tailed lizards (2.5–4 inches long) are about the same size.

Average Lifespan: Lizards can live 1–20 years, depending on the species and size.

Gila monster

Desert horned lizard

Desert spiny lizard

Mojave fringe-toed lizard

Zebra-tailed lizard

Diet: Lizards eat ants, grasshoppers, crickets, flies, worms, spiders, seeds, vegetation, flowers, fruit, and even other lizards. Gila monsters eat small mammals, as well as eggs, ground–nesting birds, reptiles, lizards, insects, and carrion.

Reproduction: Lizards lay 1–20 eggs during the summer.

Predators: Mammals, raptors, snakes, and roadrunners prey on lizards.

When to Look: Most lizards are diurnal and many can be observed racing around or sunning themselves during the day. Some are very good climbers and may be observed in trees or shrubs. Gila monsters are not seen often; early morning or late afternoon is the best time to look for them.

Most Threatening Factors: Habitat destruction is a huge threat to lizards. Gila monsters are often killed out of ignorance and by ill-informed humans. They are a protected species in Arizona.

Coping with Desert Life: Most of these species of lizards thrive in the hot, dry deserts of the Southwest! When they are not out and about, they hide under vegetation, amid rock piles, underground, in the sand, or in the shade.

Notes: Horned lizards have several survival strategies to avoid or escape predators. They can puff up like a blowfish by swallowing air, making it very difficult for predators to get a good hold on them. Some species can also shoot blood from their eyes to dissuade predators. Horned lizards also can play defense against their prey; they feed on harvester ants, which produce a powerful venom, but the lizards fire back with an antitoxin to counterattack any ant bites.

Sonoran collared lizards are excellent runners and jumpers. When running down prey, they take very long strides—up to three times their body length—and in the process they look more like dinosaurs than lizards when running.

Many lizards also exhibit "metachromatism," which means that their body color changes with the temperature. When it's hot, they adopt lighter colors, as this helps them reflect heat, but when it's cold, their coloration darkens, enabling them to absorb more heat from the sun.

Of all the adaptations found in lizards, the most famous adaptation is autotomy—a lizard's ability to lose its tail. They do this to evade predators, and the tail then grows back, taking anywhere from a month to a year to do so. The new tail consists of cartilage, rather than bone, but it's a tail nonetheless. When the tail actually breaks off, it continues to wiggle, holding the predator's interest and giving the lizard more time to escape.

In our deserts, nearly all insects are terrestrial, and they can be very abundant, but they all face a constant struggle: They must replace the moisture lost through evaporation. They have developed a number of adaptations to prevent dehydration: They avoid the worst of the heat, their body surface has a thin wax coating that decreases evaporation, and they obtain much of their water by way of metabolizing carbohydrates.

The deserts of the Southwest are also home to many spiders, centipedes, and scorpions, which all belong to a big group of animals known as arthropods. (These critters are often considered "insects" or "bugs" by laypeople, even though the term insect technically refers to a much more specific group of animals.) These creatures are well suited to desert life, and they can be plentiful.

Many of our desert arthropods are at least somewhat venomous, and they use venom to subdue prey and as a defense mechanism. While few to none possess life-threatening venom, their stings or bites can be very painful.

Taken together, the Southwest's many insects and arthropods are a perfect example of how life manages to survive—and thrive—even amid the most hostile conditions.

Giant hairy scorpion

Scorpions

(Giant hairy scorpion, Bark scorpion, Stripe-tailed scorpion, Pale windscorpion, Giant vinegaroon)

Distinguishing Features: Giant hairy scorpions have black upper parts and segments lined with yellow. The tail, legs, and pincers are yellow. The hairs on the legs, claws, and stomach are dark. The underparts are light-colored. Hairy scorpions are venomous to their prey but don't pose problems to humans. All Southwestern scorpions have pincers that are covered with tiny, sensitive hairs that help them detect vibration and movement. Once a prey item is detected, the scorpion grabs the prey with the pincers or uses the venom to subdue it.

Bark scorpions are light tan with a slender tail and pincers, and they may have yellow-green stripes above. Bark scorpions have very potent venom; bark scorpion stings are a medical emergency for those with scorpion allergies as well as the young, elderly, or people with respiratory issues.

Stripe-tailed scorpions are tan to dark brown with a striped tail. It has a heavier and larger body than the bark scorpion. Stripe-tailed scorpions are venomous to their prey, but the venom is usually not dangerous to humans.

Pale windscorpions aren't technically scorpions, but they look similar enough that they are often mistaken for them. They are yellow-brown and have large forward-facing fangs. The claws are heavy and close together (unlike in true scorpions). They also lack a long, curved tail and stinger or venom glands. Windscorpions can inflict a painful bite, however.

Giant vinegaroons (whip scorpions) are also not true scorpions. They are dark in color and have a long, whip-like tail. The front legs are longer than the other legs and used as feelers. Vinegaroons are not venomous but can inflict a painful bite.

Size and Weight: Giant hairy scorpions are the largest scorpion in the U.S. at an impressive 5.5 inches long. Bark scorpions are small and 1–1.5 inches long. Stripe-tailed scorpions are 1.5–2 inches. Pale windscorpions are 0.62–1.25 inches. Giant vinegaroons are 3–3.12 inches.

Average Lifespan: On average, scorpions live about 3–5 years, but some can live 10 years or longer.

Diet: Scorpions eat insects, small lizards, other scorpions, and small snakes.

Bark scorpion

Stripe-tailed scorpion

Pale windscorpion

Giant vinegaroon

Reproduction: Most scorpions reproduce sexually and display complex courtship rituals that even include dancing. Once mating is complete, the male quickly moves away so it doesn't become prey for the female. In the summer, scorpions give birth to live young (called scorplings), and they spend their first 7–21 days (or longer) hanging on to their mother's back and sides. Even young scorpions possess venom and are capable of stinging. But the adult's stinger is larger, packs more venom, and is more dangerous. The average litter size is 8 scorplings. Once the young go through several molts, they leave their mother and are on their own.

Predators: Rodents (grasshopper mice, desert shrews), owls, pallid bats, birds, small mammals, centipedes, snakes, and lizards all eat scorpions.

When to Look: Scorpions are nocturnal and may be observed during the summer on the ground, in vegetation piles, under rocks, in trees, under bark, in lumber piles, in moist areas, and even in houses.

Most Threatening Factor: Scorpions are often killed by humans.

Coping with Desert Life: A scorpion's outer shell is coated with a waxy substance that helps prevent moisture loss, and they can also survive severe dehydration and elevated body temperatures (up to 115 degrees). They do their best to avoid temperature extremes, taking shelter under rocks, in burrows, and in other secluded places. In summer, they seek out cool, moist areas, often making their way into houses.

Notes: If you have a blacklight (ultraviolet light), scorpions glow in the dark! They glow a vibrant blue-green, which is easy to spot. This occurs because of specialized chemicals in their skin. According to one theory, scorpions glow under UV because their bodies may be able to interpret it as light in the blue-green range; if this is true, it means their UV-reflective bodies might just serve as giant "eyeballs."

Of course, scorpions are most (in)famous for their venom, which they deliver via the stinger at the end of the tail. The stinger holds a pair of venom glands, a reservoir, and a needle-like barb. The venom consists of a mixture of toxins that are used to subdue prey but can be used for defense too. Most scorpion venom is not dangerous to humans, but a sting can cause redness, sharp pain, swelling, and some discoloration. Bark scorpion venom is the most dangerous scorpion venom from our region, and it can be harmful (even fatal) to children, the elderly, and people with respiratory problems. A bark scorpion sting should be considered a medical emergency.

Inconspicuous crab spider

Spiders

(Desert tarantula, Western tarantula, Arizona blond tarantula, Wolf spider, Apache jumping spider, Black widow spider, Inconspicuous crab spider)

Distinguishing Features: Tarantulas are dark brown on the head and legs; the stomach is brown-black. The body is hairy and heavy; there are black hair pads below the leg.

Wolf spiders are gray-brown on the head and the stomach may have a dark stripe. Females are lighter in color and larger than the males.

Apache jumping spiders are bright orange on the top of the body and have black legs and underparts. The jaws are green.

Black widow spiders are coal black with red markings on the head and abdomen. The red mark can be round or hourglass shaped. Males are light brown (and harmless).

Inconspicuous crab spiders are brown, gray, reddish, or yellow on upperparts with spots, bands, or mottled colors.

Size and Weight: Tarantulas are the heaviest and largest spiders in the Southwest, and they are 1.5–3.5 inches long. Females are larger than males. Wolf spiders are 0.75–1.37 inches long. Apache jumping spiders are small and 0.37–0.5 inch long. Black widow spiders are small and 0.37 inches long. Unsurprisingly, inconspicuous crab spiders are quite small, just 0.12–0.37 inch long. Females are slightly larger than the males.

Average Lifespan: Most spiders live at least several years, and tarantulas can live up to 20 years.

Diet: All spiders eat insects. Tarantulas also eat lizards and small rodents. The Apache jumping spider preys on small arthropods, insects, worms, and other spiders.

Reproduction: Spiders lay their egg sacs on vegetation, rocks, under bark, in a cavity, or in a burrow. The spiderlings hatch in the summer and usually don't receive care from the female. Female tarantulas allow spiderlings to hang around for 3–6 days after they hatch. Mortality is high for all types of dispersed spiderlings.

Predators: Lizards, birds, and wasps all eats spiders. In a truly horrifying example of parasitism, tarantula hawk wasps use tarantulas as hosts for their larvae, which consume the tarantula from within.

Tarantula

Wolf spider

Apache jumping spider

Black widow spider

When to Look: Most spiders are nocturnal. Black widow spiders are common in sheds, barns, garages, and human structures. Other spiders can be observed on the ground, in vegetation, on rocks, and around structures. In deserts, spiders are more active in the summer.

Most Threatening Factors: Human development, agriculture, off-road vehicles, and pesticides threaten spiders.

Coping with Desert Life: Most spiders avoid the heat thanks to their nocturnal lifestyle, and some roost underground and in between rocks to avoid the heat and cold. In addition, while many spiders generally have a dark coloration that causes them to absorb heat, dark colors also readily radiate it, which helps them cool down. Spiders also have another option; if the weather isn't cooperating, they can stay dormant for long periods, only becoming active when conditions are favorable for breeding or foraging.

Notes: Black widow spiders have a very potent venom, but they aren't aggressive. They use their venom to subdue prey and to defend themselves.

When breeding, spider females breed with one male and then store the sperm for later use. The male has to hurry though; he has no venom and must retreat immediately afterwards. If he doesn't, the female will eat him. A male's first time mating is also likely to be his last.

Spiderwebs are a natural architectural wonder. Female spiders create them to trap prey and also to making moving around easier. Spider silk consists of proteins that are produced via glands on the female's stomach. When building a web, the female chooses how strong the silk will be—it can vary for different purposes—and constructs the web in two hours or less. When complete, the web is virtually invisible but can withstand wind, rains, and the thrashing that ensues as prey struggles to escape.

Tarantulas and wolf spiders live in burrows but construct spiderwebs at the entrance of the burrows. Wolf spiders entwine twigs in their spider silk, and the black widow spider's web is irregular, messy, and very strong. Crab spiders don't construct a web but use camouflage to capture prey. Jumping spiders spin webs to capture prey and use silk to protect their eggs. Spiders also use silk as a dragline when jumping; this helps them prevent falls.

Common desert centipede

Centipedes and Millipedes

(Giant desert centipede, Common desert centipede, Desert millipede)

Distinguishing Features: Giant desert centipedes are orange with a black head and tail. They have long bodies with one pair of legs per body segment. Each leg has a sharp claw. Centipedes have a well-developed pair of antennae on the head. Most centipedes have long legs and move quickly.

Common desert centipedes are long and brown and tan in color. They also have one pair of legs per body segment.

Desert millipedes range from brown to golden-brown or a dark reddish brown and usually have bands. Each body segment has two pairs of legs. The legs are short and the movement is slow and wave-like. The body is long.

Size and Weight: Giant desert centipedes are 6–12 inches long and the largest centipede in North America. Common desert centipedes are not as large, about 4–5 inches long. Desert millipedes are large and 4–7 inches long.

Average Lifespan: Centipedes and millipedes usually live several years, but some can live 6–10 years.

Diet: Centipedes eat arthropods, such as ants, beetles, termites, crickets, grasshoppers, spiders, etc., as well as larger animals like lizards, geckos, and small rodents. Millipedes eat decaying organic material (leaves, bark, and plants) and occasionally eat living plants, leaves, and stems. Millipedes usually forage in sandy washes.

Reproduction: Male centipedes deposit sperm bundles and the females locate the bundles and impregnate themselves. In millipedes, males insert sperm via a specialized pair of legs. Females then lay eggs (10–300 at a time) in the soil or in underground nests. The eggs are covered with a sticky substance, and they need moisture and humidity to survive. Some female centipedes protect their eggs from drying out by licking the eggs until they hatch, while other females abandon the eggs. Some female millipedes remain with the eggs until they hatch and continue to care for the young until they are on their own, while others give no care to the eggs or young. Young hatchlings are small versions of the adults but have fewer body segments than adults, and they develop additional segments after each molting period.

Predators: Some beetle larvae feed on millipedes. Centipedes and millipedes are preyed upon by lizards, birds, reptiles, amphibians, mammals (coatis, shrews, etc.), and insects.

Giant desert centipede

Desert millipede

When to Look: Both centipedes and millipedes are nocturnal and more active after rainy periods.

Most Threatening Factors: Centipedes and millipedes can be found inside of human dwellings. Many are killed when discovered. Millipedes can be an agricultural pest and are killed by pesticides. Some of the larger millipedes are popular as pets.

Coping with Desert Life: Centipedes and millipedes spend three quarters of their time underground. They dwell under rocks, debris, and other objects, especially during the intense heat of summer, and they spend the nights foraging. During the winter, both centipedes and millipedes spend the entire time in a protected location (a burrow, an underground nest, under rocks, etc.) and only emerge during the spring. Both centipedes and millipedes are more active during the rainy season and prefer moist habitat. Millipedes eat moist dirt to acquire water.

Notes: Centipedes are venomous! They use their venom to subdue prey and to defend themselves. They deliver their venom by latching onto prey with their powerful fangs (which are actually a modified pair of legs), and then they kill it by injecting venom. The venom dissolves cells; thankfully, in humans it usually only causes pain and inflammation. If you are bitten, wash and clean the wound with water and soap and apply antiseptic cream. Your tetanus shot should also be current.

Millipedes have no venom and don't bite. Instead, they curl up in a ball to protect themselves. However, they can produce a bad-smelling fluid from their glands (pores) along the sides of the body. The fluid can cause an allergic reaction (especially if it gets in the eyes), and it can blister skin. As with centipede bites, wash the affected site with water and soap and apply antiseptic cream. And stay back! Some millipedes can squirt the fluid several inches!

Centipedes and millipedes lack the waxy protective coating that most arthropods have, and they can easily die from desiccation. This is one reason why both types of critters prefer secluded, dark environments.

Red imported fire ant

Well-Known Desert Insects

(Pinacate beetle, Tarantula hawk wasp, Red imported fire ant)

Distinguishing Features: Pinacate beetles (stink beetle, clown beetle) are shiny black and have an oblong body. They have 6 legs and 2 pairs of wings. The front wings are thick and form a shell over the stomach and meet over the middle of the back. The back wings are softer and fold under the front wings when not in use.

Tarantula hawk wasps are large wasps that prey upon spiders. They have blue-black bodies and rust-orange colored wings. The end of the abdomen is modified into a stinger on females. The female's stinger can be 0.25–0.5 inch in length and packs a very powerful wallop.

Their ostentatious color scheme helps warn other predators that they are venomous. Tarantula wasps also have long, hooked legs that they use to grasp prey. Males are smaller than females and lack stingers.

Red imported fire ants are reddish brown in color with a darker abdomen. They are small but very aggressive. They have 2 pairs of wings, each of a different size, and 3 pairs of legs. These ants have a small waist and a prominent stinger at the end of the abdomen. The eyes are noticeable and the antennae are bent at the corners.

Size and Weight: Pinacate beetles are 0.4–1.4 inches long. Tarantula hawks are 0.75–2 inches long. Fire ant workers are 0.12–0.27 inches and the queen is much larger.

Average Lifespan: Beetles and wasps live several months, but ants can live from 6–15 years.

Diet: Pinacate beetles eat dead and decaying organic material. Tarantula hawk wasps forage on fruit, milkweeds, mesquite trees, and Western soapberry trees. Fire ants eat plants and seeds, but some are predaceous and feed on insects.

Reproduction: Insects transition to adults via a process called metamorphosis; the female lays eggs, which hatch to produce nymphal stages that then become adults, or the egg produces a caterpillar, grub, or a maggot, which then pupates before turning into an adult. Most insects breed and develop during the rainy seasons.

Predators: Pinacate beetles are preyed upon by skunks, burrowing owls, loggerhead shrikes, and grasshopper mice. Tarantula hawk wasps are usually avoided by most predators, but roadrunners will prey on them. Fire ants have few enemies or predators.

Pinacate beetle

Tarantula hawk wasp

When to Look: Pinacate beetles are active day and night, and tarantula hawk wasps and fire ants are mostly diurnal. Insects are both more numerous and easier to see during the rainy season.

Most Threatening Factors: Pesticides, herbicides, and loss of habitat kill many insects. There are few threats to fire ants, and their numbers increase quickly.

Coping with Desert Life: Insects seek out cool, often subterranean, areas to escape the heat. Pinacate beetles have an exoskeleton that protects them from the heat. Many insects become dormant during the winter.

Notes: A mother will do anything for her babies. Female tarantula hawk wasps are powerful predators and seek out much larger tarantulas for one simple reason: Wasp larvae favor tarantulas as their food of choice! The adult female wasp locates a tarantula, stings it with her half-inch stinger, and paralyzes the much larger spider. She then drags the paralyzed (but very much alive) tarantula to her burrow and lays an egg on its back. The wasp seals the burrow and the larvae hatch and grow, all the while thriving on their living food.

The larvae avoid eating vital organs of the tarantula, prolonging the tarantula's lifespan (and time as a food source). In 250–350 days, the larvae develop into adults. Once the adults leave the burrow, the cycle repeats itself and the females are on the lookout for tarantula food for their young!

As their name suggests, red imported fire ants are an invasive species. They are native to South America and first showed up in the United States in the 1930s. They live in huge colonies (100,000–500,000 ants) and the queen can lay up to 5,000 eggs a day. Worker ants build the nest, defend the colony, find food, and care for the queen. They also pack a potent venom; they can inject a toxic, necrotizing venom that causes pain, pustules, itching, and even severe allergic reactions. Many people require medical attention after being stung, and stings happen relatively often because when ant mounds are disturbed thousands of workers emerge to viciously defend it.

In all, around 4,500 species of amphibians occur around the world, but only a few dozen are found in the Southwest. All of our desert amphibians, with the exception of toads, require access to a water source to keep their skin moist. Not surprisingly, our arid Southwestern deserts are not ideal habitat for many such creatures.

Nonetheless, a number of frogs and toads are found in the Southwest, and their special adaptations help them survive here. Many species are inactive or underground during the height of the desert heat, and some species can even sense when rainstorms are approaching (by feeling the vibration from thunder). After a storm in the desert, a chorus of frogs might just surprise you!

Great Basin spadefoot

Frogs and Toads

(Sonoran Desert toad, Northern leopard frog, Great Basin spadefoot, Bullfrog, Sonoran green toad)

Distinguishing Features: Sonoran Desert toads (Colorado River toad) are olive, gray, or dark brown in color, and the underparts are lighter in color. The skin is mostly smooth and shiny. There are warts around the edge of the mouth and on the hind legs.

Northern leopard frogs are green or brown with large dark spots, with light edges on the back and sides. Light-colored ridges run from the back of the eyes to the rump. There is a light-colored stripe on the upper jaw. The snout is pointed and the hind toes are webbed.

Great Basin spadefoots are olive to green-gray above with a white belly and red spots on the back. There are gray streaks on the back, a glandular bump between the eyes, and a black wedge-shaped spade on each hind foot.

Bullfrogs are green to brown on the back and may have darker spots. The underparts are a lighter color. The upper jaw may be light green and there are dark bands on the legs. The external ear coverings (known as the tympanic membrane) are large and impossible to miss, especially in males. The hind feet are webbed, with the exception of the longest toe.

Sonoran green toads have green or yellow-green spots surrounded by black; their underparts are lighter. Males have a dark throat.

Size and Weight: Sonoran Desert toads are large toads, ranging from 3–7 inches long. Northern leopard frogs are small frogs, around 2–5 inches long. Great Basin spadefoots are small and 1.5–2 inches long. Bullfrogs are the largest frog in North America at 3.5–8 inches long. Sonoran green toads are 1.5–2.25 inches long.

Average Lifespan: Sonoran Desert toads live 10–20 years; Spadefoot toads can live to 20 years. Frogs live 3–5 years or longer.

Diet: Sonoran Desert toads, leopard frogs, Great Basin spadefoots, bullfrogs, and Sonoran green toads eat insects, spiders, and lizards. Sonoran Desert toads even eat other toads.

Reproduction: Many toads and frogs breed and lay eggs in the rainy season. Many need standing water to lay their eggs. Once the eggs hatch, tadpoles transition to adult frogs in less than two weeks.

Sonoran Desert toad

Northern leopard frog

Bullfrog

Sonoran green toad

Predators: Snakes, raptors, raccoons, coyotes, and foxes prey on frogs and toads.

When to Look: Toads and frogs are nocturnal; they are easiest to observe after rainstorms.

Most Threatening Factors: Habitat destruction, predation, invasive species, disease, fire, global warming, drought, and urban development threaten frogs and toads.

Coping with Desert Life: Toads and frogs burrow underground during periods of drought and exceedingly warm weather.

Notes: Toads and dogs don't mix too well! Sonoran desert toads pack a powerful toxin in their skin, and they use this as a defensive mechanism. Animals that lick or bite the toad are quickly affected by the potent toxin. The toxin is absorbed through the lining of the mouth, and symptoms include foaming at the mouth, confusion, labored breathing, temporary paralysis, and convulsions! The toxin can kill a dog; if one comes into contact with a toad, it's important to rinse the dog's mouth with water from a hose and seek a veterinarian's attention as necessary. Most dogs steer clear of toads after an encounter!

Many frogs and spadefoots have powerful skin secretions that can cause allergic reactions in humans. Handling them often results in a burning sensation, sneezing, a runny nose, or watery eyes. If you touch one, you should immediately wash your hands; or, better yet, just leave them alone!

If you venture into the desert, you may not immediately see a bird, mammal, reptile, or an amphibian, but you will always see plants. The desert is home to a variety of shrubs and trees, as well as cacti, other succulents, annuals, and perennials. Each has a unique life cycle and special adaptations for surviving in the desert.

Because rainfall is unpredictable, desert plants must endure long periods of drought and incredible temperature swings. Nonetheless, they continue to survive—and thrive—and play an essential role for innumerable desert animals, providing everything from food and shelter to something as simple (but important) as shade.

Mesquite

BELIEVE IT OR NOT

Many seedlings (especially saguaro) require a helping hand when first growing in the harsh desert environment. Established "nurse plants" such as mesquite, palo verde, and creosote bush provide the shade and protection that young plants need to survive.

Shrubs and Trees

(Sagebrush, Mormon tea, Palo verde, Creosote bush/Greasewood, Ocotillo, Mesquite)

Distinguishing Features: Sagebrush is a shrub with a gray trunk and numerous branches. The leaves are green–gray and have a pungent odor. Sagebrush produces yellow and green–gray flowers in late summer to October. It's the most common shrub in the Great Basin Desert.

Mormon tea is a green shrub with numerous jointed branches and very few leaves. The flowers are small and cone–like, appearing in March or late spring.

Palo verdes are green and spiny or thorn–tipped. They are leafless most of the year. Blue palo verdes have a blue trunk, but most others have green bark with multiple trunks. The tree produces bright yellow flowers in April or May.

Creosote bush (greasewood) is an evergreen shrub with tiny yellow-green leaves that are pointed and shiny. It produces bright yellow flowers after the spring rains and, later, a fuzzy white fruit. Creosote bush is the most common and widespread shrub found in the Southwest's deserts, and it is very drought tolerant.

Ocotillos are tall, slender woody shrubs with spiny straight stems that grow straight upward. Most of the year, they lack leaves (except after rains), but from February to May, they usually produce clusters of red flowers at the tips of the branches. The flowers are tubular, 0.62–1 inch long, and attract hummingbirds.

Mesquites are spiny shrubs or trees with a short trunk, slender branches, and a bean-like pod. (They actually belong to the legume family.) Their leaves vary from green to gray-green, and the leaf size also varies. Mesquite bark is light to dark brown. Mesquites grow quickly, even with very little water.

Size and Weight: Sagebrush is 6–15 feet high. The leaves are 0.5–1.75 inches long. Mormon tea shrubs are 4 feet in height or taller. Palo verdes are 20–40 feet tall. Creosote bush can grow 3–8 feet in height and width. Ocotillos can grow 10–20 feet tall and the leaves are 2 inches long. Mesquites grow 20–50 feet tall, with leaves 3–6 inches long, depending on the species.

Average Lifespan: Desert plants are long-lived. Sagebrush can live up to 150 years and mesquite live up to 200 years. Palo verdes can live 30–150 years. Ocotillo can live for 60 years or more. Astoundingly, a creosote bush in the Mojave Desert is several thousand years old!

Sagebrush

Mormon tea

Palo verde

Creosote bush (Greasewood)

Ocotillo

Reproduction: Plants have several methods of reproduction, ranging from asexual reproduction (sprouting roots), as in some palo verde plants, to the sexual reproduction seen in flowering plants, such as cacti. Asexual reproduction creates genetically identical clones of the parent plant; sexual production produces an individual with a mix of the genes from each parent.

Palo verde and mesquite produce flowers in the spring and summer and are pollinated by bees. Palo verdes can also sprout roots as a means of asexual reproduction. Ocotillos have a long, red tubular flower that is pollinated by hummingbirds. Bees crawl around inside the Ocotillo flowers and help with pollination too. Creosote bushes are pollinated by insects but can also self–pollinate, because they have both male and female parts. Sagebrush and Mormon tea produce large quantities of pollen and are wind pollinated.

Where to Look: Desert plants are found in flatlands, dunes, washes, along slopes, rocky cliffs, amid grasslands, and in the hills.

Most Threatening Factors: Humans and invasive exotic plants threaten shrubs and trees.

Coping with Desert Life: Desert plants are experts at surviving in the harsh, dry environment! Many plants can go years without water. They also often boast "seed banks" in the soil; these dormant seeds can survive for years, ensuring that the plants will survive in spite of long periods without water.

Notes: Sagebrush may be plain-looking, but it dominates numerous desert habitats, and many animals, such as deer, antelope, sage grouse, rabbits, mice, birds, lizards, reptiles, and insects eat sagebrush or depend on it for shelter or nesting space. This makes the long-lived sagebrush a lifesaver for many desert animals.

Joshua tree

Agaves and Yuccas

(Agaves: Desert, Shindagger, Palmer's; Sotol; Yuccas: Soaptree, Mojave, Blue, and the Joshua tree)

Distinguishing Features: Agaves (desert, shindagger, Palmer's) have tough succulent leaves that form rosettes; most plants are stemless. Many have sharp, curved spines along the leaf margins and one large spine on the end of the leaf. The shape and color of the leaves vary by species, and some species have bands or spine imprints on the leaves. Most agaves flower once, then die. They can flower at anywhere from 5 years of age all the way up to 30 years old. The large flower grows on a stalk that stretches 10–20 feet from the center of the plant, and it is either spiked or branched. Flowers can be colorless, yellow, red, or purple.

Sotols, also known as desert spoons, are perennial evergreens and have dense, slender leaves with forward-curving teeth. They form stemless rosettes. Sotols don't die after flowering, but as with agaves, the flower reaches impressive proportions, up to 12 feet tall. Greenish-white flowers grow in a long cluster from the leaves.

Joshua trees are evergreen-like yucca trees with narrow, spiny, dagger-like spines. The trees also have a thick trunk and widely forked and spreading branches. The leaves are clustered together and are 8–14 inches long and 0.25–0.5 inch wide. The trunk is gray or brown, and it is rough and furrowed. The flowers are green-yellow and have an unpleasant smell.

Yuccas (soaptree, Mojave, blue) are evergreen shrubs or small trees with single trunks or clusters of them. Yuccas have a few upright branches. The leaves are long, narrow, straight, and sharp, and they end in a sharp spine. Its flowers are long, bell-shaped, and large; they are whitish or purplish.

Size and Weight: Agaves vary from a few inches wide to 12 feet across. Sotols are about 3 feet long and their leaves are 0.5–1 inch wide. Joshua trees are 15–35 feet tall and their trunks are 1–3 feet in diameter. Their flowers are 1.25–1.5 inches long. Yuccas are 10–17 feet high and the trunks are 4–12 inches in diameter.

Average Lifespan: Agaves live 10–30 years. Yuccas can live up to 20 years. Some Joshua trees are more than 1,000 years old!

Reproduction: Most agaves are pollinated by nectar bats, moths, insects, and hummingbirds. Nearly all yuccas and Joshua trees are pollinated by moths. Sotols are pollinated by bees and wasps. All of these plants produce flowers to attract pollinators.

Sotol

Agave

Yucca

Where to Look: Agaves and yuccas occur in semi-arid habitats and can be found in grasslands and on rocky slopes. Sotols grow on rocky hillsides and slopes. Joshua trees can be seen in the Mojave Desert at higher elevations and are the defining plant (known as an indicator plant) of this desert.

Most Threatening Factors: Urban development, off-road vehicles, and invasive species are threats. Javelina and deer eat young plants.

Coping with Desert Life: Agaves, yuccas, sotols, and Joshua trees have thick leaves with a waxlike coating to prevent water loss and to reflect heat. The plants also store water for periods of drought and have sharp thorns to deter predators. During the day, they close the pores that allow them to absorb carbon dioxide, reopening them when it's cooler.

Notes: Agaves, yuccas, and sotols have long been used by indigenous peoples. Fibers from the tough leaves are used for mats, sandals, nets, baskets, thatching, ropes, cloth, medicine, food (fruit and flour), fences, and even lances! Soap yuccas have a substance in their stems, roots, and trunks that is often made into soap. Various species of agaves and sotols are grown on farms and harvested to make tequila or mescal.

Joshua trees are the largest of the yuccas and are symbols of the Mojave Desert. Early Mormon travelers named them after the biblical leader Joshua; they thought the trees resembled giant humans with raised arms and were pointing the way to the promised land.

Yuccas are a perfect example of mutualism, a biological relationship in which two species are dependent on each other for survival. Yuccas are pollinated by moths, and the moth depends on the yucca for food. Each species of yucca is pollinated by one or two of its "own" species of moths. The yucca's flowers only open at one time and the moths emerge for this special event. The moth also lays its eggs on the ovary of the plant, giving the moth larvae a readily available food source.

Yuccas aren't the only plants important for other species; nectar bats time their migrations to coincide with when agaves flower.

Cereus

Cacti (Columnar and Others)

(Saguaro, Senita, Organ pipe cactus, Cereus/Night-blooming cereus, Prickly pear cactus)

Distinguishing Features: Saguaros are tall, thick columnar cacti with spiny stems. They can have several branches (arms), sometimes up to 50. Some saguaros never grow arms; the number of arms depends on the soil and rainfall. Its flowers are white and funnel-shaped with many petals; flowers occur in clusters at the end of the branches.

Senitas are columnar cacti that branch out from the base and are a green–gray color. Senitas have many branches, some quite long, while others are more truncated. No matter their size, branches have 4 or more ribs and short spines. The tip of each senita branch also has long spines. Senita branches eventually sag toward the ground, where they then root in the ground. Senita flowers are small, funnel-shaped, and light pink in color.

Organ pipe cactus has numerous slender branches that grow from a center point in the ground and curve upward. When frost kills the tips of the branches, new branches grow below the dead tips. It has small flowers that occur in white or pale lavender.

Cereus (night-blooming cereus) resemble dead sticks and are often found hidden under shrubs (which serve as protection). Its spines are small. As you might expect from their name, night-blooming cereus blooms at night, and it blooms in June; the majority of cereus bloom on only one night, but some may bloom for more than one night. It produces a large, white, beautiful flower with a unique fragrance.

Prickly pear cactus is a shrub- or tree-like plant with round or oval pads that are pear shaped. Its pads are covered in numerous spines (which are known as glochids), and the plant has jointed stems and stout trunks. Pads can be blue-green to yellow-green in color. Flowers are yellow, rose-red, rose-pink, or magenta, and the fruits are plump and reddish or purple.

Size and Weight: Saguaros are the largest cacti in the United States and commonly reach 50 feet tall, and even 60 feet in extraordinary cases. Their flowers are 2.5–3 inches wide. Senitas can be 13–20 feet tall. Organ pipe cactus can be as tall as 11 feet, but a few plants can reach almost 40 feet. Cereus can grow up to about 10 feet tall, and the flowers are an impressive 8 inches long. Prickly pear cactus is 3–6 feet in height, up to 15 feet in diameter, and the flowers are 2–3 inches wide.

Saguaro

Senita

Organ pipe cactus

Prickly pear cactus

Average Lifespan: Many cacti are very long-lived. Saguaros can live up to 200 years or longer. Senitas may live to 85–100 years or more. Organ pipe cactus can live to 150 years or longer.

Reproduction: Bees are the primary pollinator of cacti, but birds, moths, insects, and occasionally bats also help with pollinating saguaros. Organ pipe cactus is pollinated by nectar bats, such as the lesser long-nosed bat and the Mexican long-tongued bat.

Where to Look: Saguaros and organ pipes can be seen on rocky slopes that face southward, as well as on level ground. Senitas can be found

in desert flats as well as in the greener "thorn scrub" habitats. Thorn scrub habitat consists of scrubs and short trees (10–20 feet tall), and it is denser and taller than desert habitat. Cereus can be located in the desert under nurse plants, such as creosote bush, mesquite, ironwood, and other plants. Prickly pear cactus grow in well-drained soils in the desert.

Most Threatening Factors: Humans harvest and destroy many cacti. Cacti die of insect infestations, bacterial infections, prolonged freezing temperatures, and pesticide runoff from agriculture.

Coping with Desert Life: Desert plants are experts at conserving water; they store water in their stems and roots, lack the water–intensive leaves found in other plants, and they have roots located close to the surface, enabling them to quickly take advantage of any rain. They also have a waxy coating that helps prevent moisture loss, and their many spines and thorns dissuade predators from feeding on them.

Notes: The prickly pear isn't just a beautiful plant; it's a superfood, with a long cultural history. The Tohono O'odham Nation have long cooked young prickly pear pads, which are known as nopalitos. Studies have revealed that nopalitos can significantly reduce high cholesterol and blood sugar for people who suffer from diabetes.

Saguaro "boots" are formed when woodpeckers create nest holes in the towering plants. The saguaro seals the wound with scar tissue in order to prevent infection. The scar tissue forms a hard exterior, essentially creating a waterproof hollow. These ready-made habitats are frequented by flycatchers, elf owls, house finches, purple martins, and even bats. The interior of the saguaro is cool, and the boot is an excellent place for animals to stay cool or nest. Seri Indians have long used these boots to carry and store food.

Barrel cactus

Cacti (Short/Stocky)

(Cholla, Barrel cactus, Hedgehog, Pincushion, Pineapple cactus, Beehive cactus)

Distinguishing Features: Chollas are shrubby cacti with jointed stems (or branches) and sharp spines. The clusters of spines (glochids) are easily detached, and they're barbed so they're difficult to remove. The flowers exhibit a wide variety of colors, ranging from white, yellow, and green to orange, pink, violet, and even brown. The fruits are usually edible.

Barrel cactus can range widely in shape; most are barrel-shaped to columnar. They have no branches, but all have ribs and very sharp spines. Some plants even sport

fishhook-shaped spines. Their flowers and fruit grow out of the top of the plant. Flowers can be orange to red, yellow, maroon, or pink. The majority of their fruits are inedible.

Hedgehogs are usually short-stemmed and ribbed. They have a single stem or multiple branches with short or long spines. Flowers can range from bright red to rust or occur in violet, magenta, pink-red, yellow, or orange. Flowers emerge from the stems. The fruits are edible, and many are delicious.

Pincushions are not ribbed like other cacti. Instead, some plants have grooved tubercles where spines originate, but others have no grooved tubercles. Their overall shape is similar to that of a pincushion. Flowers originate from the top of the plant or at the base of the tubercles. Flowers can be yellow, pink, orange, or violet in color.

Pineapple cactus have a pineapple-like shape and numerous ribs and spines. The spines are so numerous that they hide the surface of the cactus. Flowers form at the top of the plant and can be light pink to pale white in color. The Pima pineapple cactus is endangered.

Beehive cactus is a low, stout cactus with globe-shaped stems. The central spines are yellow, orange, or brown. The flowers grow from the top of the plant and are pink, violet, or pale yellow.

Size and Weight: Chollas are 2–15 feet in height. Barrels can be 6 inches–12 feet in height. Hedgehogs are 4 inches–2 feet high. Pincushions are 4–9 inches in height and 2–6 inches in diameter. The pineapple cactus is 6–15 inches high. The beehive cactus is 3–5 inches high.

Average Lifespan: Cholla can live 30 years or more, and the barrel cactus can be very long-lived. Many of the smaller cacti are also long-lived.

Cholla

Hedgehog

Pincushion

Pineapple cactus

Beehive cactus

Reproduction: Honey bees and cactus bees are the primary pollinators of cacti.

Where to Look: Chollas, barrel cactus, hedgehogs, pincushions, pineapple cactus, and beehive cactus are common in hot deserts, but the Great Basin Desert is too cold for these cacti.

Most Threatening Factors: Cactus collectors and nurseries remove numerous cacti from the desert. Many cacti are protected by state laws. Habitat loss also threatens many cacti.

Coping with Desert Life: Cacti belong to a family of plants known as succulents, and they can store excess water in their stems and roots to use in times of drought. Their stems and branches are coated with a wax–like material to prevent evaporation, and they also have

a toxic compound in their skin to discourage foragers. They shield themselves against the heat of the day by opening their pores (to take in carbon dioxide) at night, instead of during the day.

Notes: Even though one type of cholla is known as a "jumping cholla," they don't actually jump. But their sharp joints (as well as immature plants known as "cholla balls") detach very easily, so you might not believe it if you encounter one too closely. The thorns are barbed and painful. The best way to remove the cactus joint is to place a comb between your skin and the cholla ball, then yank the cholla ball out. Once you do this, you'll soon learn to give cholla a wide berth as you pass them!

Despite the cholla's intimidating hardware, a number of bird species build their nests in them. The list includes cactus wrens, curve-billed thrashers, doves, and roadrunners, and all of them are experts at maneuvering around the prickly cholla. Packrats also use the cholla joints to protect or camouflage their nests.

Young barrel cacti and saguaros are quite similar in shape, and you might confuse the two. Thankfully, there's an obvious difference between them. Barrel cacti have spines that are curved at the ends; saguaros have straight spines. Of course, saguaros eventually outgrow barrel cacti.

Desert Life Reading List

Cockrum, E.L. and Y. Petryszyn. *Mammals of the Southwestern United States and Northwestern Mexico*. Tucson: Treasure Chest Publications. 1992.

Daly, H.V., J.T. Doyen, and P.R. Ehrlich. *Introduction to Insect Biology and Diversity*. New York: McGraw-Hill. 1978.

Dimmitt, M.A., P.W. Comus, and L.M. Brewer, eds. *A Natural History of the Sonoran Desert, 2nd Edition*. Oakland: University of California Press. 2015.

Drees, B.M. and J.A. Jackman. *A Field Guide to Common Texas Insects*. Houston: Gulf Publishing Company. 1998.

Dutton, B.P. *American Indians of the Southwest*. Albuquerque: Albuquerque University of New Mexico Press. 1983.

Fischer, P.C. *70 Common Cacti of the Southwest*. Tucson: Southwest Parks and Monuments Association. 1989.

Johnsgard, P.A. *North American Owls Biology and Natural History*. Washington and London: The Smithsonian Institution Press. 1988.

Johnsgard, P.A. *Hawks, Eagles, and Falcons of North America Biology and Natural History*. Washington and London: The Smithsonian Institution Press. 1990.

Johnsgard, P.A. *The Hummingbirds of North America, 2nd ed.* Washington and London: Smithsonian Institution Press. 1997.

MacMahon, J.A. *Deserts*. New York City: Chanticleer Press. 1992.

Nowak, R.M. *Walker's Mammals of the World, 5th Edition, Vols. 1 and 2*. Baltimore and London: The John Hopkins University Press. 1991.

Olson, C. *50 Common Insects of the Southwest*. Tucson: Western National Parks Association. 2003.

Plog, S. *Ancient Peoples of the American Southwest*. New York: Thames and Hudson. 1997.

Quinn, M. *Cacti of the Desert Southwest*. Tucson: Rio Nuevo Publishers, 2001.

Smith, H.M. and E.D. Brodie, Jr. *Reptiles of North America*. New York: Golden Press. 1982.

Stebbins, R.C. *Western Reptiles and Amphibians, 2nd Edition*. New York: Houghton Mifflin Company. 1985.

Thomas, D.H. *Exploring Native North America*. New York: Oxford University Press. 2000.

Tuttle, M.D. *America's Neighborhood Bats*. University of Texas Press, Austin.

Tweit, S.J. *The Great Southwest Nature Fact Book*. Anchorage: Alaska Northwest Books. 1994.

Wilson, D.E. and S. Ruff, eds. *The Smithsonian Book of North American Mammals*. Washington and London: Smithsonian Institution Press. 1999.

Glossary

Abdomen: the latter portion of an insect's body.

Altricial: baby birds that are blind and naked when hatched.

Ballooning: a method that spiderlings use to travel long distances. Silk strands are created and are blown by the wind, enabling the spiderlings to move from one place to another.

Carapace: the upper portion of a turtle's shell.

Carnivore: an animal that eats meat.

Crepuscular: an animal that is active in the early morning (dawn) and late afternoon (dusk).

Diurnal: an animal that is active during the day.

Dormancy: a state in which an animal does not move or grow.

Echolocation: ultrasonic sounds that are emitted by a bat (and some rodents) and that are returned to the bat as an echo; bats use the echolocation to locate prey and to detect obstacles.

Endemic: something that lives in one geographical area and is unique to that area.

Fledgling: a bird that has fledged (developed feathers) and can now fly.

Gestation: the period it takes for an embryo to develop within a mammal.

Glochid: a barb or thorn from a cactus.

Herbivore: an animal that feeds on plants.

Hibernation: a period of inactivity during cold or prolonged drought periods; during hibernation, breathing, body temperature, and metabolism are usually decreased.

Incubation: when a bird sits on its eggs in a nest in order to help them stay warm and develop.

Invertebrate: an organism without a spinal column.

Larva: the early form of an animal prior to metamorphosis and development into an adult.

Mimicry: imitating something that is poisonous, distasteful, or dangerous.

Mutualism: a relationship between two species that benefits both.

Nestling: a baby bird.

Nocturnal: an animal that is active during the night.

Nurse Plant: a mature plant that provides a young plant or seedling with shade from the heat and protection from the cold.

Omnivore: an animal that eats both plant and animal material.

Pheromones: chemicals emitted by members of the same species that are used for communication.

Playa: a desert basin that is usually dry.

Pollination: the transfer of pollen from one plant flower to another.

Precocial: a baby bird that is fully feathered and can see upon hatching.

Rosette: a circular cluster of leaves.

Rut: the period in which bucks (deer, pronghorn or bighorn sheep) fight other bucks for the chance to breed with the does.

Torpor: inactivity or dormancy.

Venom: a toxin that causes pain, paralysis, and death when injected; it may contain neurotoxins, which affect the nervous system, or hemotoxins, which harm the blood.

Vertebrate: an organism with a spinal column.

Index

Notes

Notes

About the Author

Karen worked at the Arizona–Sonora Desert Museum for more than 26 years and has extensive knowledge of birds, mammals, deserts, and animal adaptations and behavior. Her passion for hummingbirds has resulted in a book, book chapters, scientific papers, and also a husbandry manual for captive hummingbirds for the Association of Zoos and Aquariums. Her research on hummingbirds includes migration, nesting biology, behavior, song development, and longevity. Karen regularly advises zoological institutions and aviaries on the proper care and husbandry of captive hummingbirds. She has conducted educational workshops and seminars on birds for various organizations, schools, yearly bird festivals, and local bird groups. Karen has also studied bats for more than 30 years and carries out lectures and workshops about bats. Her long-term monitoring and inventory research project for bats in the Chiricahua Mountains is in its 17th year. She trains government employees on the proper protocol and handling techniques for studying bats. She has led and co-led natural history trips in Arizona, New Mexico, Texas, Mexico, Baja, Costa Rica, Ecuador, Galapagos, and Africa. Karen has a B.Sc. degree in Wildlife and Fisheries Science from the University of Arizona.